EMOTIONAL
INTELLIGENCE

An Ideology for Leaders Seeking
Extraordinary Results

DR. MAURICE L. OSWELL

Copyright © 2019 by Dr. Maurice L. Oswell.

ISBN   Softcover   978-1-950580-54-5
       eBook   978-1-950580-66-8

All rights reserved. No part of this book may be reproduced or transmitted in any form or by any means, electronic or mechanical, including photocopying, recording, or by any information storage and retrieval system without express written permission from the author, except in the case of brief quotations embodied in critical reviews and certain other non-commercial uses permitted by copyright law.

Printed in the United States of America.

To order additional copies of this book, contact:
Bookwhip
1-855-339-3589
https://www.bookwhip.com

CONTENTS

Chapter 1. Emotional Intelligence, The True Indication of Success ... 1
- Disregard I.Q. Here's the True Ingredient for Success 3
- Where Do Emotions and Logic Come From? 4
- Emotional Intelligence in the Sales World 7
- Consciousness of Emotional Intellignce 11
- Five Facets of Emotional Intelligence 12

Chapter 2. Self-Awareness 15
- Culture and Self-Awareness 20
- Real-Life Applications 24

Chapter 3. Self-Regulation 27
- Self-Regulation: Cultural Bias 31
- Real-Life Applications 34

Chapter 4. Motivation 36
- Motivation in the Face of Cultural Challenges 42
- Real-Life Applications 43

Chapter 5. Empathy 44
- Globalization 48
- Real-Life Applications 51

Chapter 6. Social Skills 54
- Social Across Cultures 57
- Real-Life Application 59

Chapter 7. More Leadership Post-EI development 61
- Coercive Style 62
- Authoritative Style 63
- Affiliative 64
- Democratic Style 65
- Pacesetting 65
- Coaching 68
- The Distinction of Leadership 69

Conclusion 71

End Notes 73

CHAPTER 1

Emotional Intelligence, The True Indication of Success

Leadership is an oft-used term that has clear significance in every arena of life—from the workplace to home. Machiavelli says in *The Prince* that, "The skill of an individual leader is the key factor in determining the success of a state or enterprise" (2003). With such pressure, the study of leadership has grown in importance, having a focus in almost every discipline. As there are countless leaders in the world, there are likewise countless ways to lead. There is no "one size fits all," clear-cut method.

To be an effective executive, most people do agree that there are certain general responsibilities that leaders should adhere to and ensure are carried out. According to Peter F. Drucker:

- The leader must understand what *needs* to be done. This doesn't mean this is always the easiest, cheapest, or the most fun option for the members of the company. The leader who excels will take what needs to be done seriously.
- Second, they think about what is best for the enterprise—again, not the employees, the leaders, or the company. To execute a project, they will do what it takes to implement it effectively.
- Conversely, a leader must be flexible about their plans. Although they may have written out a plan, it is not "set in stone" if the results are not ideal.
- Leaders must be responsible about communicating, meetings, and decision- making. Consistency and honesty are key.

- Leaders must focus on opportunities—how and where can they improve?
- Leaders listen first and speak last. When they do speak, they use the inclusive "we" as to not alienate followers.

The list isn't comprehensive, but it shows the scope of possibilities for solid leadership. Within each bullet point, a number of different responsibilities ensue, as do various ways to carry them out.

There are many characteristics that do not fall under leadership. Leadership does not equate to controlling every single task, being the one person who knows how to accomplish every aspect of a business in an obviously right fashion. Rather, leadership is motivating a team and delivering a vision to best execute goals (Gupta 2009). Guidance under a leader ensures the creation of a goal, a road to that goal, and—importantly—to know *people* well enough to organize and meet the goal successfully.

The latter is arguably one of the most important. After having a number of leadership positions in life, this quickly becomes apparent. If you ask any employer, communication skills are usually valued as the number one most important skill in the workplace. If you go online, website after website lists "verbal communication skills" as a primary skill that employers repeatedly seek in their candidates. In fact, according to the book *Cultural Intelligence: Living and Working Globally*: zzzzz [block quote] Many organizations regard social skills or interpersonal skills as key qualifications for new employees. Upward of seventy percent of most managers' time, in most cultures, is typically spent in interaction with others—superiors, subordinates, peers, clients, and others—in face-to-face conversations, meetings, telephone calls, and informal social settings.

(Thomas et al. 2009) zzzzz-end block quote

Knowing how to interact spans just about every area in the workplace. Not only do employees and particularly leaders communicate frequently, but the act of communicating with others actually dominates the bulk of the day's time. This is a time- consuming yet extremely important responsibility. As *Cultural Intelligence* goes on to ask, "How can any task be carried out, how can leaders delegate responsibilities, and how can delivering a vision to a team successfully occur without a clearly communicated message?" (Thomas et al. 2009). Carrying out instructions influences the employees' understanding and thus, the whole project. Have you ever been part of a project, perhaps in school or at work, and you have no idea what the instructions are? Maybe you've paid attention to the lectures, but the professor's head was in the stratosphere and he wasn't clearly delivering his lesson. You're left confused and unable to start anything at all.

In the workplace, a project is also driven by a vision, and having this vision drives a business and really, any endeavor. If this vision is the motivating force and the leader is the liaison for communicating its delivery, it's important that the leader can communicate with clarity and understanding to make this vision come alive for the business. If it is communicated well, the chances of everyone being on the same page are increased.

When someone is passionate about an idea, it's apparent to the listeners. It also grips the attention of the audience. Monotone, Ben-Stein speakers who sound hesitant, apathetic, or like they'd prefer a nap won't be able deliver any sense of the vision.

Disregard I.Q. Here's the True Ingredient for Success

If communication is so important, then what in turn leads to successful communication skills? The interesting fact is that leaders can "get through" to coworkers better with a greater understanding of emotions. Communicating and implementing tasks effectively are the result of two skills: the first, *knowing yourself* well. The second, *knowing how to interact* with the people you work with—not just knowing how to do your job.

Plenty of people have "know-how:" you go into a profession because you're good at that particular subject. Obviously, scientists are good at science; engineers excel at math. Having the abilities to perform the job itself is unquestionably important. However, one can optimize their performance in the workplace with knowledge of not only processes and information, but also how to facilitate the process by working effectively with people.

Too often, people equate success with I.Q., which is a disappointing road. We've all had that brainiac in class who wins all the academic awards, who we imagine going to MIT, being the next Bill Gates, and having millions. We assume that because they have the intelligence, they will succeed in the workplace. Nobody can increase their I.Q.—it's set in stone by genetics. Intelligence and capability for knowledge, this "know how," is beyond our control. But what if I told you that there *is* another means for success? That, in fact, I.Q. *isn't* the best indicator of potential success at all? Startlingly, people with the highest I.Q.s often have a significantly lower rate of success. This is contrary to popular belief yet true.

As posited by psychologist Daniel Goleman in his book *Emotional Intelligence*, the true indicator for success in any given field is actually Emotional Intelligence, or EI (1997). Emotional Intelligence encompasses a range of skills that harness an understanding of your own emotions and the emotions of others. Salovey and Mayer (1990) defined Emotional Intelligence as "the subset of social intelligence that involves the ability to monitor one's own and other's feelings and emotions, to discriminate among them, and to use this information to guide one's feelings and actions" (p. 189).

While knowing how to do your job effectively is, of course, a necessity for those in leadership positions, it isn't enough. Studies have shown that leaders lacking in emotional intelligence underperformed by an average of twenty percent, whereas leaders who exemplified the various characteristics of emotional intelligence outperformed yearly goals by fifteen to twenty percent (Goleman 2000). That is pretty remarkable. It would seem that Emotional Intelligence is worth our time to investigate.

Where Do Emotions and Logic Come From?

Harnessing our Emotional Intelligence is not just sensible in reality, but our bodies naturally act upon emotion. We are emotional beings who try to justify our actions by rationalizing, and this is a scientific fact. In our brains, the limbic system controls emotions. Everything that we taste, smell, see, and touch goes through this limbic system before it reaches the prefrontal portion of our brain, which is the section of the brain that is responsible for rational thought. Our bodies must understand outside stimuli from an emotional perspective before rationalization can occur. For instance, you walk down the street and see what appears to be a snake. Instantly, your palms become sweaty, your mouth goes dry, and before you have a chance to look and see if it's really a snake or just a piece of rope, you're afraid. If it looks like it's a snake, you run away or emit a shriek. This is a prime example of the limbic system's reign in the brain; in that momentary lapse when you sense danger, rationalizing is out of the question. Even if the fear and scream lasts but a second, logic is secondary to our natural emotional impulses.

Interestingly, Goleman's explanation of the evolution of the brain elucidates this phenomenon. "The primitive brain," as he calls it, is comprised of the brain stem. This controls the most basic processes in our bodies, pain sensory, breathing capabilities, and basic survival functions of that nature. Such brains still exist in life forms such as insects (1997). What arose next from the brain stem is the emotional portion, from which the thinking portion then grew. Evolution itself speaks to the dominance of emotion over logic.

If the limbic system is the "emotional" brain, then the neocortex governs the logical aspects of the brain. If you try to learn a new skill, such as how to speak a language or how to learn Java for your computer, the neocortex is heavily involved. When businesses try to train employees in the art of Emotional Intelligence, they tend to use activities that utilize the neocortex rather than the limbic system in the brain. This misses the point entirely. Daniel Goleman states that the limbic system learns best through "motivation, extended practice, and feedback" (2011). Learning Emotional Intelligence, then, is not as simple as providing a how-to handbook. It's a hands-on experience that thrives from practicing working with people, not studying facts as you would with a test. Also unlike a test, Emotional Intelligence Training cannot be standardized. Each of us has a measure of Emotional Intelligence, but the areas that need improvement vary from person to person and in different measures.

Even research studies point to greater activity in brains that reason emotionally.

One research study examined brain activity while respondents were asked questions about workplace dilemmas. Greater activity is shown in more parts of the brain when there's an emotional reaction, the ones that rely on "gut feelings" (Gilkey et al. 2010). The best strategic thinkers employed various parts of the brain, such as those that anticipate other people's reactions, and had significantly less focus on the prefrontal cortex, or the area responsible for appraisal, assessment, and other such logical functions (Gilkey et al. 2010). This should call for employers to evaluate situations with a wider lens, as more of the brain is lit up when it works in conjunction with emotions, rather than just in the logical prefrontal cortex. Thus, thinking emotionally taps into a greater capacity to think universally and engage more of the brain. This maximizes brain processes and activity when searching for solutions to everyday problems.

Unlike I.Q., Emotional Intelligence is encouraging in that it *can* be improved. It is not a predetermined capability engrained in our DNA, it is a collection of skills that can be explained, practiced, and mastered. If working well with others is an ingredient for success as well as an acquired skill, then success itself is acquirable as a practicable skill. This brings hope to leaders. Because their overall intelligence is a static feature, emotional intelligence is refreshing as a group of skills that can be practiced. It is noteworthy that many individuals ar more prone to characteristics of emotional intelligence, but that doesn't mean it cannot be improved with practice. Indeed, emotional intelligence tends to increase with age and maturity (Goleman 2004). But even with maturity, people benefit from training in emotional intelligence.

Think of it this way. We have a team of engineers who must collaborate on devising a solution. They clearly are brilliant; that is unquestionable. The problem is that they often work solo, bent over a desk, poring over papers. They may be accustomed to relying on their own expertise but not in a group. Knowledge is their strong suit, but typically, they're soft-spoken or perhaps don't know what proper team dynamics should be. To carry out their task, knowing how to collectively identify the problem, discuss the nature of the problem, evaluate a possible solution, and embark on the plan for the solution, they must have an awareness of how to work together. If they have the knowledge but don't know how to collaborate and communicate together to carry out their job, then what use is the knowledge in the first place?

Emotional Intelligence in the Sales World

Knowing how to work together is crucial in just about any sector of the business world. Increasingly, businesses are vying for consumers' attention, claiming to have an unparalleled product or service. While so many advertisements flash before our eyes on television, zoom by on the highway, and sneak their way onto the medium of print, one must wonder: is Business A really selling anything more superior to Business B? After all, everything appears the same after awhile.

In actuality, sales are more than tangible transactions. As many companies sell similar (or the same) products, a business distinguishes itself subconsciously in the minds of customers in regards to its humanity: how is the customer's *experience*—not just the objective exchange, but also the personal exchange? How have the employees succeeded in going above and beyond the expectations of the customer/business relationship?

Take this example: John walks into the Apple Store one day to peruse Macbooks.

He's about to graduate, and to his delight, his grandfather had mailed him graduation cash. "Yes!" he exclaims. "That's definitely going toward my college laptop." He's already had his eye on an Apple per his friends' recommendation. "Mine is just as fast as the day I got it," his friend had told him.

The problem is that John doesn't know much about what he's doing. He walks into the Apple Store, and the sales associates are stationed respectively at the cash registers, store entrance, and beside the gadgets in the store. The greeters do their job robotically. "Hi there, welcome to the Apple Store." Another employee dusts the monitors as he walks by, waiting for someone to ask for assistance.

John hesitates before giving a few computers a test drive. He moves the mouse, taking the computer out of sleep mode. The desktop background is a leaf with dewdrops on it, and the picture is pristine and bright. He clicks a few buttons, trying to identify the Internet search engine, and at last finds the elusive search bar. Upon surfing the web a while, John witnesses the speed of the computer. *Pretty sweet,* John thinks as he's transported from one webpage to another in almost no time at all—vasty different from his old desktop.

Knowing a Macbook is right for him, he thinks about asking the opinion of an employee. Unluckily for him, the employees on the floor are facing one another against a table, chatting about the night before.

"I was like, 'What the heck are you doing here?' She's been so crazy lately…" "Right?"

"She needs to get a grip on herself."

The other employee nods and leans toward the other employee. They don't seem to notice John on the sales floor, and their body language suggests that they're only interested in the subject of last Saturday night. Not wanting to interrupt them, John considers shopping by price.

"Is this going to be all for you today?" Asks the cashier when John walks up with his uncertain decision.

"Yeah," John says.

The transaction continues in silence as the cashier scans the box, clacks on the keyboard, and says, "That'll be 2399. Credit or debit?"

John walks out of the store, bag in hand, and the job of securing a laptop is done.

Nothing remarkable about the experience, no real connections made. The employees were unaware of the visible emotions on John's face. While this scenario does accomplish the bare minimum in job-related tasks—the greeters greeted, the cashier worked the register, and so on—it lacks any emotion.

By contrast, creating a customer experience as opposed to a simple customer visit goes as follows…

John walks into the Apple Store and is instantly greeted. "Hey there!"

"Hey," John replies.

"What are you out shopping for today?" asks the employee.

John is able to express his interest in a laptop for college, and the employee (who introduces himself as "Mark") nods his head and leans in, showing concern for John's needs.

"Alright, well those are actually going to be right over here. The difference to keep in mind between the Macbook Air and the Macbook Pro is..." Mark trails on, using the computers to demonstrate their various unique features. John can tell that Mark is paying attention to if John seems to be following, asking questions to ensure he's not confused, and overall, personalizing the sale. Mark consistently makes eye contact and is engaged with John.

"Here's one of our Mac desktops," says Mark, gesturing to a computer the size of a decently large television.

"Oh, that's big..." John says, not explicitly stating that he thinks it's over the top, but it clearly shows on his face.

"If you're looking for something more space efficient, we have this array over here," says Mark, guiding him to another row of options.

Between discussing the various options, they casually chat about more general topics.

"I'm just glad I don't have to worry about antivirus software as much. We had a desktop at home that kicked the bucket after only a couple of years."

"Yeah, I've had a PC die on me too only about two years after I got it." Mark commiserates with John.

Mark pays attention to what John could need in college, such as a sturdy laptop case for protective transport, as well as a wireless mouse. Continuing to converse at the cashier, Mark finishes his sale.

"Well, I'm certain your grandpa will see that his gift went to a good cause," Mark says.

"For sure! I'm excited to set this up. Thanks again," says John. He then walks out of the store, feeling confident about his purchase.

To make the most of a sale, leaders and employees alike in business must be aware of how the *customer experience* plays into success. This is just one area that benefits from an understanding of Emotional Intelligence.

When products stagnate in copious advertisements, when simple efficiency in transaction is not enough, the customer service becomes pivotal. Remaining in the customers' minds is not the satisfaction of the simple obtainment of the product, but the specialized treatment by the employees. The customer should feel a sense of empathy from the exchange, a sense of importance, even pampering. Mark specialized his exchange with John by keeping his college needs in mind, guiding him throughout the store, and personalizing his dialogue (such as mentioning Grandpa). As the old saying goes, one is more likely to complain of a terrible experience than rave about a good experience. Anyone can provide the bare minimum in a sales transaction—"Here you go, that'll be 9.99" as the only interaction—but to truly stand out, employee development behind the business scene is a necessity.

Businesses will not thrive to their fullest potential by training employees that are only task oriented. Rather, they will reach their fullest potential with *people-oriented* employees. For this reason, leaders in the business world, particularly a sales environment, must train emotionally in-tune employees to go above and beyond and keep the customer for the long-term. Knowledge of Emotional Intelligence accomplishes this ideal end-goal.

Emotional Intelligence offers a unique way to assess the less-black-and-white areas of a person's capability. Rather than the Intelligence Quotient, or I.Q., the measurement of one's intelligence, Emotional Intelligence, judges one's emotional awareness, the ability to identify, understand, and harness one's emotions. Having emotional intelligence is having the ability to read another person's emotions, whether subtle or blatant, in a variety of situations. Whenever John's face revealed a hint of puzzlement, Mark saw this and decided to slow down, be clearer, and utilize the store's laptops on display for clarification. Sensing an emotion is not enough; identifying what that emotion is, evaluating it, and acting upon the evaluation is another important part of EI success.

Mark may have thought, "Hmm, this person looks sort of dissatisfied. They're frowning. I don't know why, though. Oh well," and resumed his chatter on the wrong laptop (this would truly be obtuse). However, thinking back to earlier, "I remember John saying he doesn't like very large computer monitors, maybe I should place this back on the shelf. He probably feels reluctant to listen to what I have to say because I come across as only trying to sell him something, so I need to try a different approach. I need to show I care about his personal consumer needs."

Consciousness of Emotional Intellignce

This doesn't only involve interactions with others, as depicted earlier. Emotional Intelligence is also an internal regulator, an ability to gauge emotions within. From this, an analysis of your emotional state leads to an evaluation of how your actions will be affected by this emotion. Adjustment of how to handle this emotion and how to proceed will follow.

For instance, a group member makes a rude remark at work about your job performance. You may think, *I'm angry right now, and I'm probably going to do something rash. I feel threatened and nervous at the idea of failing at my job. Instead of yelling, let me consider why my coworker thinks this, and how I can manage to understand this person's perspective right now.* (Thinking with this measure of clarity might be unrealistic initially, but you could think one of these thoughts as a head start for emotionally intelligent thinking). First, you identify your emotion—in this case, anger.

Trying to understand why your first instinct is to lash out at your coworker in anger is the second step—identified as insecurity about job performance. Then, converting that anger into a desire for a solution follows: how can I better understand my coworker and why they feel this way?

It's easy to let animal instincts triumph and carry out that feeling (whether it's anger, fear, nervousness, and so on) without regard to its cause and how to monitor it. After all, you're caught up in a primal sensation—fighting against emotion to think about reason and logic in counterintuitive. Understanding a wide range of your emotions and knowing how to utilize this mindfulness, though, is what guarantees success.

Five Facets of Emotional Intelligence

Think back to the examples of people who are mindful of their emotions and how to wield them. Think about the people who are not only introspective, but easily understand and interact with others. What do these various instances describe? The aforementioned illustrations describe the five essential components of Emotional Intelligence: self-awareness, self-regulation, motivation, empathy, and social skills.

Using just one aspect of emotional intelligence is beneficial, but harnessing the aggregate of skills altogether truly yields an effective leader.

Self-Awareness is just as you'd expect: being aware of your self. Self-awareness involves introspection of strengths, weaknesses, desires, goals, annoyances, habits, and characteristics along those lines. This is a general understanding of what emotions you're prone to, how others affect your emotions, and how you affect others. For example, you know you're a monster when you have too many tasks to attend to in a short period of time. You lash out at people and curl up in a ball at your desk. Self-awareness is your ability to come to terms with this and sense its wearying effects. Not only that, but self- awareness is particularly vital in cross-cultural interaction. To understand where another person comes from (in a cultural sense), you must first be aware of your own culture.

Then you can see how this culture is similar or different to your own and know how to best respond to it.

Self-regulation is an understanding of how to control these behaviors, and, as the name suggests, *regulate* them by choosing when and how to respond to these emotions. Self-regulation is the knowledge gained from self-awareness, such as knowing your tendency to stress out. As mentioned, you recognize that you are easily stressed. To regulate this tendency, you buy an agenda and plan when to work on each assignment, making these "freak-outs" a less common occurrence. This can also be when you count to ten and breathe rather than yell at someone when you're upset.

Motivation is the unending desire for accomplishment. While you may envision motivation as a driving force for a higher salary and words of affirmation, the motivation here is different. Motivation is seen when an employee demonstrates a desire to learn, a passion for improvement for improvement's sake. The prospect of being the best you can be is sufficient motivation. Likewise, you wish to motivate others. To successfully motivate a team, you best achieve this by utilizing the other aspects of EI.

Empathy is a very familiar form of emotional intelligence. It's popularized in the phrases "Put yourself in somebody else's shoes," "Before you judge somebody, walk a mile in their shoes," and the plethora of similar phrases (often involving shoes). Empathy is important in matters of race, cross-cultural sensitivity, and gender. If you admit that your reality is not an unquestionable truth and that it is worth understanding another human being, the harmony in the workplace increases.

Finally, Emotional Intelligence includes social skills. Although this sounds like the ability to get along with everybody you encounter or going out and getting drinks with coworkers, social skills entail more than that. Possessing social skills is the ability to move people toward a goal—very similar to the concept of leadership itself. Social skills are about building relationships and managing those relationships.

As touched upon earlier, one skill often trickles into another (without self- awareness, how can one utilize self-regulation, for instance), and social skills certainly utilize a blend of empathy, self-regulation, and the other components. Although these skills may seem obvious for success, masterfully blending these skills and knowing when to use them is not so simple—which is why emotional intelligence training exists in the workplace. When put into practice, though, collective utilization of these ideas can give you previously unparalleled success.

Therefore, the challenge of a leader is not simple mastery of knowledge on their given subject. Truly successful leadership doesn't mean you are solely a jocular, likable person. Though social skills are important, one who is wholly emotionally intelligent incorporates all aspects. It does involve the ability to facilitate the completion of end goals. But as we learned, it's more than that. Leaders should not only know their limitations, but how to cope with them. Leadership considerations include fostering effective communication by being receptive to the feelings of others in order to best create a collaborative environment. Where feelings of trust and understanding abound, so does productivity.

Leaders must also understand that successful management is not about selling the most. It's about creating a workforce that produces results. So often, leaders strive to change people. If the focus is on changing other people, there will be disappointment. A more fruitful approach is to change how we interact with people, not the people themselves. As with Mark, being adaptable to each situation by personalizing communication, paying attention to nonverbal cues, and having an awareness of John's probable feelings led to success: John's certainty that his purchase was well informed.

When people take this open-minded approach, they will see the results they desire in the workplace, at home, and anywhere they go.

This isn't to say employees won't change at all as a result of emotionally intelligent leaders. We know that a smile is contagious. When leaders are positive and aware of how their moods and actions affect employees, the trickle-down effect occurs. When leaders know how to interact with their workers, there is more satisfaction. When they are honest about their strengths and weaknesses and are confident in how to cope with them, workers feel they can do the same. In leading by example, leaders promote an overall more efficient, positive workplace.

The following chapters go into depth about each element of emotional intelligence. If you practice each skill and truly understand what they entail, all of the aforementioned benefits will enter your life. Also keep in mind that you must *want* to learn Emotional Intelligence (Goleman 2011). If somebody doesn't want to learn how to ride a bike, chances are they won't learn. The same goes for Emotional Intelligence. If you want to see the changes that Emotional Intelligence can potentially bring into your work environment—and your personal life, it will require practice, practice, practice.

Once you devote yourself to the practice, watch your productivity soar, as well as the morale of your employees.

CHAPTER 2

Self-Awareness

It's interview day. You see your reflection in your shoes, your suit is crisp, and you've brushed your teeth twice to rid of coffee breath. You gather your portfolio to tuck in your hot-off-the-press résumés, and you review interview questions to yourself so you don't forget and stare dumbly for a minute after the question is asked. Your preparation and the insight of your answers will be sure to wow employers.

"'What has been your biggest challenge?' Easy, working as a shift manager at the toy store because I picked up the slack of the never-present bosses." You shudder at the memory. "My greatest achievement? Hopefully employee of the week isn't too cliché.

"My greatest strengths: organization—to be honest, I'm a little anal. Communication—I love to talk, and I'm darn good at it—and finally, I am a quick learner. Weaknesses: I procrastinate, I don't apply myself when I'm not sufficiently challenged, and I can be a little impatient."

There they are—the age-old interview questions: "What are your greatest strengths?" and conversely, "What are your greatest weaknesses?" Seemingly an unavoidable interview question, many people can rattle off their finest (and not-so-finest) qualities off with no hesitation. You've cruised to a great start to the interview, having aced the questions (carefully crafting responses to possible interview questions was a good idea, after all!), but the question is, what is the significance of these questions, anyway? Is it just to test the interviewees to see if they respond with answers already in all interviewers' minds?

The fact is that these questions gauge your self-awareness. Companies want to know if you are capable of introspection. They want to know if candidates can assess themselves honestly and recognize patterns in their behavior. That's what self-awareness is all about: what are your strengths, weaknesses, habits, goals, dreams, capabilities, values, interactions, and how do they affect your ability to get the job done as well as collaborate with other people? It's about if you can name these emotions in yourself and others and understand these patterns. Of course, naming strengths and weaknesses is just the tip of the iceberg. It's also important to know what to *do* with this awareness.

Self-awareness is helpful in myriad ways. Knowing what your strengths are and where you're most likely to succeed increases confidence. When your superior presents you with the opportunity to tackle a project perfectly suited for your skills, you can take it confidently. "I want to give that presentation because I know my public speaking skills are excellent," you say. Likewise, if you know public speaking isn't your strong suit, you graciously decline the offer. Or, if you are aware of your weaknesses, you find ways to improve upon them and gain exposure. It's not a problem to have weaknesses, after all.

It's important to know how to cope with them and what to do with those weaknesses. If you're considering jobs and know that you have no patience for people, then customer service probably isn't the niche for you. Assessing yourself accurately shouldn't be an intimidating, negative process because it guides you in making the best possible future decisions for yourself.

Because self-aware people know their failures, they aren't surprised if they are given unfavorable feedback. They channel their shortcomings into a self-deprecating humor—this is a hallmark of self-aware people. Judge when it's appropriate to use this sense of humor; if you're lower in status or use it too often, you may just seem too hard on yourself or depressed. However, those higher in the business or successful people use this and receive good reception for it. That's because it's like a device for humility.

Keep in mind that when discussing weaknesses, make sure you don't present a *fatal flaw*—that is, a flaw that "jeopardizes the central aspects of your professional role" (Goffee et al 2000). For instance, if you want a sales job and you tell the employer, "I am painfully shy—I always like for other people to make the first move," and "I don't like to work with people," then chances are that you won't be hired because being confident and generally enjoying human interaction is an integral part of sales. If you're terrible at the primary job responsibility in the role you seek and make it known, don't expect to be hired. But also keep in mind that without being open about your minor flaws, people will invent flaws for you (Goffee et al. 2000). If you reveal your weaknesses, it shows that you're human and aren't perfect; everybody has an area in which to learn and improve.

This is honest and respectable to people around you.

If a company has employees who are unaware of themselves, results can be disastrous. This can be likened to a couple arguing—not to mention self-awareness is applicable in this arena of life as well! The wife has a new puppy that wreaks havoc on the house, a clumsy yellow lab that hasn't quite grown into his paws. The puppy ran around outside, rolling in the mud and digging in the flowerbeds. He then ran inside and tracked mud all over the new white carpet (why the owners decided to put in new carpet at the time they bought a new puppy is beyond our comprehension). Predictably, the husband is irate.

"This g-d dog needs to go! He's been nothing but a nuisance!" The husband is clearly raising his voice, turning red, and eventually yelling about how much he cannot stand this dog any longer.

"Stop yelling at me!" says the wife. "I'm not yelling!" yells the husband.

"Are you deaf? If that isn't yelling, I don't know what is."

Rather than dealing with the situation directly, the wife is distracted by her husband's inability to perceive how jarring his manner of speaking is. A successful fight (if you can measure fights as successful) involves speaking as calmly as possible, being very aware of your emotions, such as your wish to lash out, and knowing how to phrase the dialogue—"You're being completely irrational" as an ineffective accusation versus "I feel like it's very hard to talk with you right now." A lack of self-awareness leads to a standstill, as shown in the fight.

Now, notice how self-awareness in this scenario might work out: "It always makes me feel bad when you yell at me," says the wife.

The husband stops talking for a moment, knowing that in past situations he has been notorious for yelling. He might say, "Let's just talk about this later and focus on cleaning up." He knows he's too angry to be constructive, and it's best to take care of the muddy tracks on the carpet first.

When a lack of self-awareness occurs in the workplace, it's just as harmful in the leader/employee relationship as with a husband/wife relationship. When communication is crucial, as it often is at work, such an ineffective communication scenario will prevent solutions.

Take Mr. Jones. During his secretary's birthday, he walks by her desk and says nothing.

"Would you like a cupcake, Mr. Jones?" his secretary holds out the box to him.

"No. I don't like cupcakes." He speaks gruffly and pushes away, not even wishing her a happy birthday. Not focusing on his lack of manners, well wishing regarding her birthday, and formalities such as "No, thank you" instead of an outright "No," Mr. Jones is preoccupied. He's thinking about a rather unsuccessful conference he just experienced instead. Although this is an isolated incident of a lack of self-awareness, it leads to the secretary's bitterness and a bit of gossip behind the copy machine.

"What's up his you-know-what today?" she whispers to a friend. "I don't know. He's being crass," she reassures.

Unfortunately, there's no shortage of leaders who lack self-awareness beyond an isolated incident. Managers hired based on work performance and intelligence may be brilliant but lack the insight to know how they come across during interactions. They may be pondering their to-do list, like Mr. Jones, rather than considering the feelings of others. They may dive into their work and ignore the opportunities to get to know their coworkers and, quite possibly, are just oblivious most of the time. This leads to a lack of trust and even fear from the employees. "I'd rather not go talk to him about my problem because he won't think it's a big issue," "I don't want to bother him or waste his time," "I don't want to deal with his anger," are all thoughts related to a manager who lacks self- awareness.

This prevents employees from bringing important details to a leader's attention. It also prevents these problems from being dealt with effectively.

This is why there are interview questions that try to measure emotional intelligence, such as the standard strengths and weaknesses question. Other questions are designed to see if the person is aware of what they could have done better in the past—such as "Name a time you experienced failure." The objective isn't to trap you into stating your shortcomings so much as to see how you objectively analyze yourself and learn from the past.

For example, in a comparison of two candidates for a job, the Harvard Business Press article "Hiring for Emotional Intelligence" depicts a self-aware candidate favorably: "the candidate concluded by saying that she had thought a lot about what went right and wrong in the project and how she could be more effective the next time she was called on to contribute to such a project." By contrast, the other candidate repeatedly said, ""I knew I was right—the others just refused to see it'" (Bielaszka-DuVernay 2008). The first candidate is thoughtful, dwells for a healthy amount of time on opportunities for growth, and shows that she isn't deterred from taking on responsibility in the future. The second candidate perceives herself to be right under all circumstances, appearing oblivious. This is not a helpful stance to have in fixing problems.

Generally, the good signs in interview responses are that the candidate is aware of the emotions surging in their head at the time and demonstrate an ability to control them. The bad sign is when the candidate fails to acknowledge a connection between emotions and behavior and frames oneself as a victim rather than demonstrating an openness to change in the future (Bielaszka-DuVernay 2008). Awareness of these red flags helps employers recruit the best possible employees. Rather than focusing on sole accomplishments, interviewers that ask these questions and look out for answers that designate emotionally intelligent candidates will acquire a more successful workforce.

Of course, to recognize characteristics of Emotional Intelligence requires emotionally intelligent employers. Leaders who are not self-aware would only escalate conflict and lack the knowledge on how to improve employees' awareness as well.

Culture and Self-Awareness

Self-Awareness is vital as it pertains to culture. Not only must you know your tendencies, you must know your culture and its relation to other cultures around you. The workplace is becoming increasingly diverse; you would see Asians, African-Americans, Caucasians, Hispanics, Middle Easterners, and plenty of other ethnic groups if you were to scan the cubicles at work. But skin color is only the tip of the iceberg, if not entirely irrelevant. Cultures are rich and complex. So many cultural systems govern the day-to- day lifestyles of humanity, and there are many sublevels to culture. Not only do you identify as an American, but you also identify with more specific groups.

Think about your own life. You live in the United States of America. Your culture values efficiency and apt time management. You probably take the drive-thru at McDonalds rather than leisurely walk there to take an hour-long breakfast with the whole family. On that note, you drive more than you walk or bike ride. The average household is nuclear: two parents with two kids, more or less. You won't often see twelve extended family members in one household. Grandma and Grandpa have their own house, perhaps a few states away. Your parents expect you to be out of the house and on your own by your early twenties (not to mention you want to be gone. You couldn't handle living with your parents into your thirties, no way). You seek your future with only yourself in mind—no need to seek approval from every family member before you apply for a job.

People live by the phrase "the world is your oyster." The workplace primarily values job performance. The list goes on and on, but this is the cultural lens through which you view life as an American.

But there are other subcultures you fit into within that culture. Perhaps you're not just an American, but you're a northeasterner. You speak with a Yankee accent, saying "sweethaht" rather than "sweetheart." Maybe you're a southerner, and you unfailingly hold the door open for women. Maybe you're from Texas…but Texas is a big state comprised of countless cultures. There's the more cosmopolitan north Texas "DFW" area, and there's the stereotypical West Texas where people may actually ride horses.

Houston is the fourth biggest city in the United States, so there are numerous cultures within that one city itself. Frisco and Plano are both cities in Texas, but the cultures of the two Dallas suburbs still differ even though they neighbor one another. Plano might be viewed as a more upscale than Frisco, and Frisco may be seen as more diverse and family oriented.

As you can see, there are plenty of subcultures already from a regional analysis.

The part of the country down to the neighborhood in which you live usually vary culturally. However, there are subcultures based on personal characteristics and hobbies. Tennis aficionados are distinct from diehard football fans—and even the moms differ!

Soccer moms and dance moms have their own distinct culture. The culture of a well-off teenager differs from that of a sixty-five year-old in an impoverished neighborhood. Each group to which that person belongs has its own set of beliefs and practices.

Seeing how culture is such a presence in everyday life, it is important to explain culture and its significance. Social scientist Geerte Hofstede describes culture as consisting of "shared mental programs that condition individuals' responses to their environment" (Thomas et al. 2009). The view of culture as a "program" is notable because it depicts how interwoven you are with your culture. Your own culture is implanted in you, it constitutes who you are, and it is thus extremely difficult to shake off your sense of culture. Your personal cultural context molds you and your perceptions of the world. This is why, when a student studies abroad, they experience "culture shock." This different way of life that surrounds them is unnatural to what they're accustomed to; it contrasts with their own internal programming. The context of their sense of self within a group is changed, affecting their sense of self entirely.

Culture is intrinsic to the self. It lies between the unshakable human nature—such as sexual desire—and personality, which varies on an individual basis (Thomas et al. 2009). Culture is unlike the ubiquitous human nature and the unique personality; it focuses on groups, is shared, but has variations among the separate groups. In viewing culture as *programmed* within you, as Hofstede suggests, the difficulty of understanding another culture becomes apparent. Looking past your cultural practices and understanding that there *are* other ways of living can be a jarring experience—it goes against your wiring, after all. That is why different cultural practices seem foreign, odd, or just plain wrong to you. Plus, there are so many cultures and subcultures in the world that it seems like a fruitless task to try to understand each one…and it is, so I'm not advocating that. Rather, *awareness* of the main categories in which cultures differ is beneficial here.

For instance, there are gauges to measure the various aspects of culture. These gauges help with drawing comparisons and understanding the way other cultures operate. You can look at cultures in the level of gender equality they exhibit or how often they make familial considerations, i.e. do eople in this culture view themselves as part of the collective group (in-group collectivism), or as a single individual? Sense of humor and modesty are other gauges. Which type of humor is appropriate in this culture, and which is not? For example, the dry humor of Britain isn't as prevalent in America. Other cultures may not understand sarcasm. In China, modesty is highly valued. When a woman has her friends over for a lunch party, she will fret about the food quality and put herself down. The expectation is that her friends will bring her up and will say, "Hush, I'm sure your food is wonderful. It always is!" Cultures also place different emphasis on what is considered inappropriate for television. Europe has no problem with nudity, but European tolerance for violence is a lot lower than in America. Knowing general categories and how different cultures fit into them helps identify trends among them and serves as an excellent starting point in cultural intelligence.

Israeli psychologist Shalom Schwartz mapped a long list of cultures according to such gauges. He and his team identified three universal requirements of a culture: the way it connects to the natural world, its need to preserve itself, and how individuals relate to the society as a whole. Cultures carry out these requirements in ways that often differ from culture to culture. However, Schwartz found seven values that fit into the requirements of a cultural framework. These include: egalitarianism, harmony, embeddedness, hierarchy, affective autonomy, and intellectual autonomy (Thomas et al. 2009). These values address the aforementioned universal requirements, showing a culture's relationship among societal members (hierarchy, embeddedness, egalitarianism) and its environment (harmony, mastery, and autonomies).

Again, I'd like to note that it is not feasible to memorize the key characteristics of every culture you're likely to encounter. But understanding the key values mentioned above, and the level to which a differing culture abides by each value compared to your own culture, is immeasurably helpful in creating not only self-awareness, but a cultural awareness as well. You can study up on these prior to meeting a member of that culture. Looking at Schwartz's map, you can distinguish how Middle Eastern nations have a more structured social hierarchy than the United States. In more traditional middle eastern countries, men are the leaders of the house hold, and women have different, specific expectations that do not include the pursuits that men have available to them. In Morocco, a woman should never walk around publicly without a male escort. That wuld be taboo in Moroccan culture. In measuring other values, the U.S. is a nation that pursues intellectual autonomy compared to South American nations, which heavily values family and thus has a higher level of embeddedness. Decisions are made in the best interest of the family in Mexico, whereas in the United States, family is often less of a consideration than personal passions and pursuits.

In sum, it is insufficient to have self-awareness in regards to your personality traits and habits. Be aware of your culture. Know what your cultural values are; know how your values may be similar or different to another culture. Look at Schwartz's map to view your culture's traits in relation to others. In understanding your culture, you will understand why you perceive other cultures in the way that you do. You can more easily identify stereotypes, which in turn will help you work them out and discover what the truth actually is. You will become a more flexible leader in doing so. In an increasingly diverse workplace, your self-awareness in regards to culture will only be an asset to your business and daily interactions. Understanding or having knowledge of different cultures has a positive impact on one's ability to effectively lead people from different backgrounds.

Real-Life Applications

The pharmaceutical industry, especially in sales, is a dynamic and competitive environment. As with any sales industry, it is fast paced and has a high turnover rate. If you are supporting a family, securing that sale and earning that commission as soon as possible becomes almost an obsession. Accurate self-awareness is not only a matter of importance because of its long-term value, but a matter of time and money. Products in pharmaceutical sales are exhausted quickly, needing rapid replacements. Those who are able to self-coach or self-assess based on appropriately identifying their strengths and weaknesses are more readily identified by their customers as credible. Thus they realize better results—which is important in a commission-based income.

As a leader in the pharmaceutical industry—leading people in general—I found it essential to set an expectation that people self-coach. In other words, as a leader I was transparent about being conscious of what I was good at while acknowledging what I still had yet to learn. This proved prudent because of the aforementioned fast-paced nature of the environment, as well as the trust you gain from the customer.

But self-awareness is also important in people's relations in any industry. I try to be open and honest while coaching pharmaceutical sales representatives and display awareness about my shortcomings. This in turn allows sales reps to open up about their own shortcomings, and we can more quickly work toward solutions for improvement as well as motivate one another.

My job looks something like this: for approximately two-to-three days out of a six-week period, I drive around to sales calls with twelve representatives for coaching purposes. Their job is to share plentiful information with the doctors to try to fit our products into their treatment algorithms. I'd observe, then ask about how it went. In the back of my mind, though, I'd wonder: *What do these times look like while I'm not with my reps? Are they as effective when I'm not with them?* Whenever you have a boss critiquing you, you probably give the sale "your all." I also wondered if they were taking me on what we call "Milk-runs," or taking their leader to the customers with whom they have the best relationships.

Although these thoughts crossed my mind, the *most* important aspect of their experience is not my presence increasing their motivation, not the feedback I give to them, and not even the sales. The most important aspect of this experience is what the sales reps are capable of achieving on their own. It didn't matter what they said to the customers that day. It was more important to me what they did in terms of self-coaching, *how* they self-monitored after the customer interaction. I am proudest when they verbalize the aspects of the sale that needed improvement.

In order to do this, my sales reps have to be able to take themselves out of the situation. They have to be able to evaluate and be honest with themselves.

"I really could have done a better job, and this is how…" "My plan was not the position's plan."

"I needed to allow him or her to proceed with his or her agenda." "I was too headstrong. I forced my agenda on him or her."

To better explain these opportunities for improvement, sales representatives oftentimes struggle on selling someone. While they may blame it on a faulty sales pitch, not being friendly enough, or the like, this is a matter of knowing how their own self- awareness affects the physicians to whom they propose sales. Reps who are clueless about what went astray probably have a difficult time explaining how they impact other people, not just themselves. That's where people have to work specifically. It is insufficient to be aware of yourself alone. Rather, how do your strengths and weaknesses impact other people? How does having a "driver" personality impact other people? Are you Type-A? Are you able to change someone who is not a driver? *Can* you change someone with that particular personality?

In any occupation or career, this is an applicable idea. If you're Type-A (as I am), this can work for you as strength or weakness. Two Type-As will probably clash, so be in tune with your self. If you're a Type-A and you sense that your customer is too, then don't fight for that top spot in the situation. Give some time to the customers; hear their perspective instead of immediately thrusting your two cents down their throats.

Also on an interpersonal level, self-awareness of your strengths and weaknesses can secure the trust of others and increase your credibility—both of which will increase your leadership effectiveness. The customer doesn't want to see you as an infallible selling machine. If they identify with you as a fellow human being, they will also see that you're also a customer who could potentially be in their situation. Then they know that you are trustworthy as a fellow consumer.

By modeling habits of good self-awareness, you help to create a more self-aware organization. An organization that is self-aware is open to learning and better equipped to adjust quickly to changes as the marketplace dictates. And as we know, the market is never static. Adaptable, ever-changing employees gel with the equally ever-changing environment. This gives a competitive advantage to your organization.

CHAPTER 3

Self-Regulation

Mike is facing the frustrating scenario of an unmotivated team. He checked in on his team members earlier in the week, asking how their tasks were coming along.

"It's going fine." "Yeah, I've got this." "No worries."

After such confident responses, Mike decided he could trust each one of them to fulfill their duties. But now it's a day away from the deadline, and panicked responses flood in.

"Mike, I need help with this data set." "Hey how do you do..."

"Sorry, I was a little busier this week than I had anticipated, so I didn't complete..."

Mike smacks his forehead with his palm. The fact his teammates request help isn't the issue. Rather, it's that the nature of their questions are rudimentary. They should have figured out these questions earlier! This means they aren't far into the project at all. Mike then wonders how long it will take them to actually get through the main portion of the project if they're stuck at this early juncture the day before the deadline.

The only excuse is laziness, thinks Mike. He is tempted to type out a strongly worded email to the whole team, reprimanding them for their procrastination and apathy. Instead, he takes a walk to cool down and returns to his computer. What is done is done, and now it's time to ensure his temper doesn't botch the project further. Instead, he formulates an email that asks them what has been diverting their attention to the project, does there need to be an extension, and questions to amass more information before he makes assumptions. Maybe he had overloaded them this month—who knows?

In this scenario, Mike redirected his emotions. His first instinct is to rant and rave and label them as lazy procrastinators. After some calmer consideration, he decided to inquire further and ask why they're only just now able to complete the task. After all, if everybody is behind, maybe the lapse in judgment is his, not theirs. Overbooking his employees isn't unusual.

Self-regulation is related to self-awareness, but describes more specifically the ability to control emotions, whether negative or positive, in order to maintain a demeanor best suited for professional practice and activity. Goleman writes about self-regulation not only as a reactionary approach to scenarios that can jostle, excite, and distract, but also as an executive's steady and deliberate impact on organizational culture: why does self-regulation matter so much for leaders? People who are in control of their feelings and impulses—that is, people who are reasonable—are able to create an environment of trust and fairness. In such an environment, politics and infighting are sharply reduced…

Talented people flock to the organization…and fewer bad moods at the top mean fewer throughout the organization (Goleman 1998b, 3).

The idea that executives shape the tone and attitude of interpersonal behaviors—and, consequently, productivity—in an organization is not a new one. Goleman also emphasizes the direct correlation between self-regulation and ethics, indicating that "people with low impulse control" (Goleman 1998b, 4) sometimes succumb to threats to integrity. "A propensity for reflection and thoughtfulness" (Goleman 1998b, 4) exhibited by the leader of an organization, then, offers security to every area affected by leadership decision-making, particularly staff and finances.

While self-awareness places emphasis on internal awareness, self-regulation emphasizes social norms. Opposed to simply knowing yourself and your tendencies, self-regulation dictates that you recognize the social climate, what is acceptable and what is not in, a given situation. Self-regulation is adaptation. People should adjust themselves to the context at hand. Scholars state that "this ability to adapt to the social context through self-regulation allows emotionally intelligent individuals to remain functional team members," not just in everyday circumstances, but, "even when faced with membership turnover, membership conflicts, or other situations that might prove detrimental to overall team organization and effectiveness" (Prati et al 2003). This is similar to Mike's dilemma. He had to adapt to the problem by looking within himself and considering other options for coping. The new context wasn't ideal, but Mike had to examine the problem and chose to self-regulate in light of setbacks.

When considering if self-regulation is necessary, use this as a guideline: zzzzz- [block quote] Unless the behavior is a difference that makes a difference (i.e. in safety, legality, or productivity) work to understand it. Change your behavior.

Instead of dictating a set change in the employee's conduct, engage them in thinking inclusively, connect with them to explore their intentions, identify the potential impacts of their behavior and develop better alternatives.

("Emotional Intelligence: A Promising Pathway to Inclusion" 2010) zzzzz-end Furthermore, leaders must have sensors: when they harness their self-awareness and identify weaknesses, they also must know when it is best to share these weaknesses. They must "collect and interpret data" (Goffee et al. 2000) to sense when the best moment is to share these weaknesses. This goes for just about any activity. Leaders must engage their sensors to interpret their surroundings. The current climate of an organization reveals when this moment is.

Many people view their opinions and understanding as the only reality. As difficult as it is to break that sometimes-subconscious state of mind, it yields positive results to truly work to understand where others come from. When coworkers seem incompetent, apathetic, and whatever other negative quality that you judge them to have, it pays to "explore their intentions," as stated. We are not omniscient beings. It is possible to be completely wrong. Even if you're not wrong, no harm ever came by talking together calmly about what had occurred and how to best find solutions. Therein lies a main idea of self-regulation—holding off on judgment of others in order to best carry out a solution.

What Mike discovered after processing his emotions and deciding to be open minded is that he actually did overbook his employees, having assigned projects earlier in the quarter that had the same due date. That didn't mean that his employees weren't apologetic and trying their best to get it done. They did show regret, and a couple of them said that it wasn't an excuse, but in the end, Mike set back the due date. If Mike had blown up (as was his first instinct), this would have alienated his workers and created resentment. Instead, he harnessed his frustrated emotions to figure out why he was frustrated and why this could be occurring.

This brings us another important point of self-regulation: to self-regulate, you must be comfortable with change. As stated, self-regulation is a form of adaptation. Effective leaders use self-regulation to monitor their emotions and the actions that result from them. This leads to exploration of solutions either alone or with a team, as occurred with Mike. Because self-regulated people have control over their emotions, they can comfortably transition between these changes. Flexibility, then, is a hallmark of self- regulation.

Adaptive change is a form of flexibility needed in self-regulation. Leaders with adaptive capacity are defined as having "the resilience…to engage in problem-defining and problem-solving work in the midst of adaptive pressures and the resulting disequilibrium" (Heifetz et al. 2009). In spite of external and internal conflict, a self- regulating leader digests the nature of the problem and how to figure it out, setting aside emotions and being open to various possibilities. As with Mike, having the necessary conversations is important in spite of how uncomfortable they may be. To best define the nature of the problem, gathering all pertinent information is needed—such as the perspective of the employees.

To enact adaptive change is an uneasy transition, as implied above. This involves stepping outside of your comfort zone much of the time, and sometimes by being flexible, taking an approach that isn't your first choice. Chapter twenty of *The Practice of Adaptive Leadership: Tools and Tactics for Changing Your Organization and the World* states, "Leading adaptive change requires you to step beyond your default behaviors into an unknown situation and to learn something new. That means experiencing a period of incompetence" (Heifetz et al. 2009). It goes on to define the nature of adaptive change: "if you do not feel that you are operating at the very edge of your talents or even just beyond that edge, then you are probably not attacking an adaptive challenge." By trekking into these unfamiliar situations, you're learning something new about your leadership, problem-solving abilities, and character. The unpracticed moments that stretch your thinking help you grow more than in the comfortable, everyday scenarios.

From the lower end of the spectrum, incompetence, you only have room to grow to unprecedented heights. After experiencing incompetence through adaptive challenges, a leader gains "guts," so to speak.

Self-Regulation: Cultural Bias

Manager Jennifer is talking with Marcelo about the possibility of his transferring to another branch of the company in order to take over a leadership position there. He would make a great fit; his resumé is impressive and he's been working at the company a long time. Yes, it requires a transfer, but the pay increase is a plus. In this tough economy, who would argue more money? Jennifer explains the situation and gives a packet with all the details to Marcelo. He shifts in his seat and doesn't radiate the excitement that she expected from him.

"I trust you will have no problems in this new role. The Cleveland branch would really benefit from your expertise," she explains. Marcelo sits there, casting his eyes downward.

"Well, does this sound good?" Jennifer asks.

"I need time before I give you my final answer." Marcelo looks concerned.

Jennifer shakes it off, noting that Marcelo has always been stoic compared to some of the other employees. Maybe he just hasn't processed the good news. She's sure he will appear more chipper as time goes on and as he reads the informational packet.

The next day, she checks her email and sees that Marcelo sent her a message late last night. In short, he said, "I appreciate your interest and trust in my abilities. At this time, for the sake of my family, I cannot accept your offer." He thanked her again. He was ambiguous, so Jennifer doesn't understand why or how he could turn down such an opportunity. She knows he has four children, and having more money to support children is never unwanted. Before she knows it, she starts to judge Marcelo. He's from Chile, so he must be a "lazy Latino." Maybe he doesn't want responsibility. He is probably satisfied with the bare minimum of work, just enough to get by.

Had Jennifer displayed self-regulation in regards to stereotyping, she would have refrained from such judgments. Self-regulation takes self-awareness into account, and the same idea applies to self-regulation in cultural awareness. If Jennifer knew about South American culture, she would have known that it emphasizes in-group collectivism, meaning the level of loyalty to a group, such as a family. They also have a higher level of uncertainty avoidance, meaning they like to control the future and rid of uncertainty when possible. These are just a couple of auges to compare Chilean culture with American culture, gauges that are relevant in this situation.

Marcelo actually turned down the job for a couple of reasons: he helps take care of his mentally retarded uncle, he has a large family including four kids, a wife, and his mother—who is elderly and also lives with them, and isn't familiar with that part of the country. With so many family members (some requiring extra care, as with his uncle and younger kids), taking an uncertain leap into unfamiliar terrain did not appeal to him (not that it would appeal to him anyway). He worried about the logistics of moving, the unfamiliarity of this part of the country and finding new doctors for his uncle and mother, and his family's unwillingness to move. The kids loved their school; his wife enjoyed this area. Plus, they've lived here for ten years. Having the extra responsibilities at work would affect his presence at home, which could be problematic considering the circumstances. Family triumphed, and he decided to stay put.

It is not unlikely that some Americans would have turned down the job as well.

However, Jennifer judged him based on his different cultural background. While Chileans do share certain values as a culture, values that Americans may view as odd, that does not make them wrong. There is no "right" or "wrong," just different.

Unfortunately, people too frequently perceive differences as wrong, odd, and foreign. This is because they are viewing other cultures within the lens of their own cultural framework. Jennifer, who stereotyped him as a "lazy" latino, came to her conclusions about Marcelo based upon the ignorance of that culture, as well as the beliefs of her own culture that value efficiency, amassing more wealth, and following one's individual dreams over the interests of a collective. Marcelo didn't appear to have the same values as those derived from Jennifer's own culture.

To be successful in the workplace and especially in leadership, you cannot view other cultures within the confines of your own cultural values. In Marcelo's culture, he is taking the right course of action. It is Jennifer's job to regulate these thoughts, wonder why she's thinking them in the first place, and find a way to understand Marcelo's perspective better. Self-regulation in both the cultural and universal sense requires *identification* of the feeling or action (or self-awareness), and an *analysis* of this feeling or action in order to *evaluate* a better outcome. In this case, Jennifer would catch herself judging Marcelo and his decision (the identification stage), would then analyze the situation—such as through consideration of Marcelo's culture and personal circumstances, and evaluate herself and the next steps in her job searching process. She would understand that she has a propensity to stereotype, and could make the decision to study cultural intelligence and familiarize herself with basic tenets of other cultures that she regularly encounters.

As can be seen, self-regulation extends to the realm of cultures. To reduce discrimination, bias, and misunderstandings in other cultures, one must self-regulate. This is not just an individual activity. It affects relations with other people who may be harder to understand due to differences in basic beliefs and practices. These differences may unleash frustrations, biases, and a lack of self-control in those that are working with other cultures. Self-regulation is even more critical in these interactions because it's so easy to misinterpret others. Under the duress of confusion and the habit of looking at people according to the constraints of your own culture, self-regulation is a test of strength. If leaders display a sense of self-awareness in regards to culture and can regulate themselves to avoid unwanted misunderstandings and tense relations (which is fairly common in cross-cultural interaction), then they will truly be effective, strong role models in the workplace.

Real-Life Applications

The concept that resonates most with my background and experiences, especially in sales and marketing, is the impact that self-regulation has on integrity. When an organization goes through changes that force people in the organization to change the way business has to be done, self-awareness and self-regulation are two key attributes that have key roles in how effectively these changes occur. If a company has done business with a certain level of fluidity—where little regulation was involved—and suddenly they are inundated by policies that are perceived to limit their ability to earn as they did in the past, integrity can be comprised.

People want to believe that leaders are making changes and saying the right statements because of outside influences. Therefore, some people are willing to compromise the rules for what they believe leaders really want for the betterment of the business. Leaders must be able to redirect disruptive behaviors to ensure the high integrity performance and values of their organizations.

Looking back at the pharmaceutical industry in the 1980s, it was like the "wild, wild west." We took doctors to the Bahamas and on various international trips, we gave them ham and turkey at Christmas, and paid for gasoline when gas was high—all for the sake of making a sale. We weren't regulated at all. In this time period, pharmaceutical salespeople could have invited thousands out to eat. It was about winning over the doctors—not so much about the product as it is today.

But around the late 1990s and early twenty-first century, people became more aware of our marketing practices as prescription drugs skyrocketed in cost. The government scrutinized pharmaceutical salespeople and our practices; they thought it was time to crack down. We weren't doing anything wrong—none of our practices were against the law—but that was just how we conducted business. However, patients started wondering if doctors were prescribing high-cost drugs just because of these large pharmaceutical companies.

Self-regulation came into place here. We knew we couldn't continue with what others perceived as gaudy practices. Now we faced the ultimate test of self regulation: no one was regulating us in our day-to-day activities, enforcing government officials weren't present in our very office, but we were expected to regulate ourselves and severely scale back on our generosity in sales calls. Many sales representatives took it as more of a guideline: *if you can get away with it; do it.* Leaders around this time had to be the ones who took a stance. They made the decision of if they would say one thing at the podium and then continue to perform these taboo practices under the table.

I personally wanted to move away from the perception that we were doing immoral activities to get doctors to prescribe our products. Self-regulation still is about doing the right thing regardless of internal or external pressures. It is necessary to redirect those disruptive behaviors that may cause you to sacrifice the values and integrity of the whole organization. It's not just about you—your actions reflect on the aggregate of the company representatives. I knew we needed to feel good about ourselves because we made the right decision internally.

Now all sales representatives can do in the pharmaceutical industry is take doctors out to lunch because of the strict guidelines in place. The trips, the money, the free stuff—all these perks fell by the wayside as the value proposition shifted to the patient and their potential benefits from the product. Deciding to make this shift was the result of self-regulation. In this way, you can see the undeniable link between integrity and this facet of Emotional Intelligence.

CHAPTER 4

Motivation

Every day, Melissa wakes up at five o'clock a.m., silencing the blaring alien-invasion noises that emit from her alarm. She peeks out her window to look at the pathway. A drape of darkness hangs over the terrain still; the only light is a faint white fog barely creeping from the horizon. She puts on her Nike shorts and knots her shoelaces before grabbing a slice of bread from the kitchen on her way out the door. When she steps outside, the air instantly chills her to the bone. *I should have put on a long-sleeved shirt*, she thinks, but figures that she'll eventually generate enough heat to where it wouldn't be necessary anyway. She breaks into a jog, and sure enough, the sweat comes anyway.

A half-hour passes, and three miles are complete. She alternates sprints and easy jogs. The conflicting feeling of having a numb face and extremities while having a sweaty body is a slight annoyance, but she treks onward, even though the blister on her heel may have broken and is giving her trouble. By this point, more of the sun manages to break through the dusk, lighting her path.

Another hour passes, and Melissa finally approaches her house, glistening with sweat and congratulating herself on her progress. The sun has risen and the land is aglow, as is her spirit. Just a couple more weeks until the half-marathon, and she feels confident that her hard work will pay off when she manages that feat. For now, though, it's off to class to take that calculus four test—after a shower, of course.

Melissa goes through the day effectively considering she woke up at five o'clock a.m., feeling energized from her physical activity. She devotes her entire attention to the lectures and concentrates hard on her exam.

After class, she comes home to study—even though a nap sounds ideal at that point. Eventually, she goes to bed at ten o'clock p.m. and will wake up the next day and start the whole schedule over again.

For people who don't enjoy working out—let alone running for intense distances, let alone at the crack of dawn—Melissa must seem crazily motivated. Surely there's the motivation of losing weight, or maybe her parents are on her case about her grades not showing her full potential. Why did she choose to run a half-marathon, anyway? Maybe she's motivated to win because of a cash prize. Maybe a boy she likes is doing it too.

Plus, a large chunk of her college friends wonder who could study all day after such an early morning. She must really need that A in math. The possibilities for motivation are endless, but the fact is that Melissa is simply a motivated person through and through. She enjoys running for the sake of running itself—the benefits of physical fitness appeal to her; plus, she likes to empty her mind and use the repetitive motion of running as stress relief. Her daily run is her thinking time, her "me" time. The half-marathon is a byproduct of her enjoyment of running. She enjoys the challenge, and she figures she could run one in time with such a passion for the recreation (even without consciously following a half-marathon preparation program). As for the studying, she applies the same line of thinking to school: she enjoys the challenge. She wants to live up to her highest potential because she just can't stand it if she doesn't. It's a waste, plain and simple. She doesn't need her parents to tell her that.

The type of motivation that Melissa portrays is inherent to emotional intelligence. As Daniel Goleman explains, motivation in an emotionally intelligent context is when a person wants to achieve for achievement's sake (2004). While money, recognition, and other forms of rewards are often great motivators for people, this motivation results from driven people who just want to see their best (or others' best) efforts succeed. Motivated people revel in their achievements as worthy of celebration alone because their greatest potential is unlocked and successfully engenders positive effects.

What happens when a leader is motivated in this way? When love of the task at hand is evident, there's a deeper commitment to company goals. When leaders are motivated by money, the job gets done (and perhaps done well), but the process of getting there is different. Leaders who are motivated often demonstrate a love of what they do. As Goleman states, these leaders "seek out creative challenges, love to learn, and take great pride in a job well done. They also display an unflagging energy to do things better" (2004). Tasks aren't simply job requirements. They provide an opportunity to grow. They provide a chance to demonstrate capability and the strengths of everybody involved. Failure isn't pure failure, it's a nudge to an alternate pathway to success. This motivation in turn motivates the employees: "If you set the performance bar high for yourself, you will do the same for the organization," (Goleman 2004). Surrounding yourself with driven people in turn accelerates your own drive for success.

Taking on this healthy perspective motivates the employees in turn; this mode of thinking creates a sense of optimism. If a leader is motivated, he or she tends to be optimistic, which in turn creates a trickle-down effect. This is due to a phenomenon called mood contagion, which, according to new research, "shows that a leader's emotional style also drives everyone else's moods and behaviors" and is likened to the phrase "smile and the whole world smiles with you" (Goleman et al. 2001). It shouldn't be surprisingly because moods *are* contagious—if somebody is cracking up good- naturedly, it's uncommon that they're met with stone-cold stares (maybe in the wrong situation, but generally this is a safe assumption). If somebody smiles at you, you don't want to be rude and fail to smile back. This simple transfer legitimately improves mood because the simple act of smiling can trick the body into being happy (Stibich 2010). So, it is no wonder that leaders who greet people with smiles, are pleasant, or are simply aware of how their emotions impact others create a more positive working atmosphere.

Contrast this with an atmosphere in which leaders are oblivious of how they come across. Emotions that ensue may range from anger to confusion. When leaders nurture a mood of optimism and/or cheerfulness, the environment is in turn more motivating.

Employees wish to succeed. They want to please the leaders that they respect. If the leader is in an awful mood, subconsciously employees may think, "Well, nothing can be done to please that guy, anyway. Why even try?" Thus the environment of an optimistic, motivated leader is more open, trusting, and productive as a result (Goleman et. al 2001).

If leaders aren't motivated, the mood-contagion effect and an open environment cannot occur. Additionally, "Because authentic leaders need to sustain high levels of motivation and keep their lives in balance, it is critically important for them to understand what drives them. There are two types of motivations—extrinsic and intrinsic" (George et al. 2007). What follows is a balancing act between the two. Enjoying the respectability, recognition, and rewards (also known as extrinsic motivation) is perfectly acceptable. We would be lying if we said we didn't enjoy these fruits of our labors. Extrinsic motivation is necessary. But to truly do a job well done, intrinsic motivation must be present. It propels us when extrinsic motivation seems out of reach. Intrinsic motivation gives your life value, meaning. Finding that niche and running within its framework is gratifying to those who are motivated by what they do.

You can add to less superficial extrinsic motivation by surrounding yourself with a team that boosts your morale and with which you can mutually support and motivate one another. From that, intrinsic value ensues: "No individual achievement can equal the pleasure of leading a group of people to achieve a worthy goal" (George et al. 2007). The gratification of not only leading yourself to success, but others, exponentially increases with each person on the team. It feels good to succeed and achieve a goal, but it feels better to see each person also take pride in the collective achievements.

Interestingly, other facets of Emotional Intelligence feed into motivation.

Although possessing motivation, a successful leader in EI is also self-aware. Without an awareness of strengths, the confidence to pursue achievement is not present. Weaknesses and limitations also need to be recognized. In order to attain achievement, failures will occur. Knowledge of what could be improved, what succeeded, and what areas of your own personality play a part in these setbacks and successes helps drive you on your path with a new awareness that is necessary for future achievement. After all, if you can't look within yourself to learn from your mistakes, they're just that—mistakes—when they *could* serve as second chances instead.

Take Joanna, for example. She is a new independent business owner of a profitable custard store. During the summer months, as one would imagine, business is as hot as the weather. Lines go to the door and, if people don't mind standing outside, past the door and around the corner. She has many unique custard concoctions and a family- feel to her store that sets it apart (knowing many customers by name doesn't hurt, either). The novelty of her creations and her charm, as well as the store's, help give her large profits during that quarter of the year.

Fall comes. Sales decrease, and less people crave the cool treat. Winter doesn't fare better—in fact, Joanna suffers quite a loss. She has to let go a good portion of her employees, and the ones left aren't as available they had been during the summer.

Paychecks go out to her remaining employees later than usual, and taxes are harsh. Even though the morale of her workers is low, they are motivated by her can-do attitude. She is a pleasant manager to work with, even if times are tough, and she certainly loves her store. Joanna always greets her faithful customers by name and doesn't hesitate to give them coupons every so often. Beyond managing her employees, she takes a genuine interest in the happenings in their lives and has built rapport with them.

Throughout the ordeal, though, Joanna keeps her chin up as she constantly thinks, there's *always* something to improve. She gets out her notebook and pen and brainstorms ideas for next year. *Hmm, fall,* she thinks. *What is a hallmark of fall that can reel customers in?* The answer is quickly apparent: Halloween and the pumpkin flavor. She marks on her checklist that she should inquire about pumpkin custard recipes—artificial flavoring doesn't pass at her custard store. Nutmeg and pure pumpkin should be added, if possible. For Halloween, she wants to consider something to reel in children. A black chocolate custard with chocolate bats? Planning to also consider her budget for these ingredients, she thinks about how this will all fare in the grand scheme of things.

Football is huge during fall and winter, so she decides to cater to football fans. Discounts on big game days sound like a plan—perhaps a two for one deal, or buy one get one half off. Who said custard isn't a football snack to rival wings, anyway? After the game day discount idea, she realizes she can apply the same concept to basketball too. A March Madness special would coincide nicely with the end of winter. Feeling confident that times will improve and that she has learned from her poor performance, Joanna rests easier during the end of the troublesome winter.

Summer rolls around again, and business is as profitable as the summer previous. You don't have to try *too* hard when you provide a cold treat in ninety-something degree climates! Joanna gains enough money to hire a new team, also because she needs them anyway when the store is constantly busy. Joanna extends her summer hours to closing at ten p.m. to closing at eleven p.m., helping profits further. Needless to say, business returned.

Thankfully for Joanna, her motivation paid off, literally. When she introduced her new concepts of pumpkin custard and game day specials, it caught on quickly. This is due in part to her advertising efforts during the summer, letting customers know, "Look out for a new flavor in September!" Of course, she took into consideration that cooler temperatures will mean less customers overall, so that was to be expected. However, after football games, she was pleased to see many jersey-wearing alumni and students frequent her custard store, excited for the buy-one-get-one deal. The pumpkin flavor was a hit, boasting real-pumpkin flavor like a pie grandma would make. Joanna felt pleased with herself for being resourceful and motivated to change her status quo.

If Joanna were merely motivated by money, she might have taken her business elsewhere. But she was passionate about her existing profession in her local custard business and decided to work with these problematic external aspects of the business. Knowing the nature of her problem and knowing that, while much of it is outside her control (colder weather just isn't as conducive to custard sales as hot weather), she learned she *could* at least mitigate the situation with creative solutions. As time went on, she was motivated to do even better, knowing that there's always room to improve. She created a catering menu and even introduced custard birthday cakes—eventually, photos could be printed on them. There's always more innovation to consider.

As can be seen, emotionally intelligent leadership does not mean that the leader is devoid of flaws or mistakes. It's how one copes with these mistakes, critically thinks about them and how to change them, that defines a motivated leader.

Motivation in the Face of Cultural Challenges

In engaging with other cultures, people experience confusion and misunderstandings; it's a fact. Staying motivated in the midst of these problems is tough. Motivating people of other cultures can be an even tougher challenge—what motivates people who originate elsewhere and possess other values and customs? Those who are both emotionally and culturally intelligent are great motivators because they are able to read different cultural gestures and body language.

For example, Aubrey works to secure a sale to an Asian firm. Throughout the duration of her sales pitch, the people in the room are seemingly meek, and their stoic demeanors are unchanging—even at the points that Aubrey views as "cinchers," where they should jump on the offer. Looking out at a sea of unexcited faces is jarring to mostly anybody else. But Aubrey knows that the set of customs in this part of the world has its own rationale, even though it is not immediately obvious to an American such as herself. Keeping this in mind, she stays motivated. She decides to approach the sale from another vantage point and notices that, if she looks deeply enough, their faces subtly light up. She keeps rolling with this new change of pace. Although they are still relatively impassive, she is motivated enough to see that their gestures are more springy and energetic, and their eyes are more alert. Gathering that their motivations are different, she knows how to approach these sales for Asian firms in the future, tossing her initial attack of the plan.

She also learned how modesty and meekness play a part in their culture.

On that note, emotionally intelligent leaders also realize that what motivates an American (say, money) doesn't necessarily motivate someone in another culture (such as recognition of improvement over time, family time, etc). A motivated leader will seek out what motivates the people in each culture, which may be vastly different. They realize that even though this is difficult, it is worth it to invest such time and effort. Thus the motivation is multifaceted: be motivated to learn what motivates others, even when it's not entirely obvious.

Real-Life Applications

Being driven to achieve for the sake of achievement became my "war cry" as a sales leader in the pharmaceutical industry. In the early 2000s profit margins begin to shrink, the FDA became increasing cautious about the safety profile of drugs. Big Pharma was also being evermore scrutinized for their direct-to-consumer advertising as well as for close financial relationships that had developed with key opinion leaders in the medical field around the word. Not to mention that the Pharmaceutical Industry had decided to self-impose marketing guidelines to change the perception of the value proposition being offered to the physicians.

Unfortunately, once all of the "shiny offerings" (i.e. meetings at nice resorts—dinners at restaurants with their spouses, etc.) were taken from the healthcare practitioners, what was thought to be the perception turned out to be reality.

Pharmaceutical sales people had been able to give these "shiny offerings" on sales calls to further their case. Once this became strictly limited as a result of new guidelines, many physicians did appear to value the stuff more than the science. However, it wasn't because they did not care about the clinical information that supported the drugs, but because many sales representatives learned to leverage promotional items. These changes impacted the way sales people were evaluated and thus incentivized. Leaders had to learn how to get their people motivated to achieve purely for the desire of achieving.

The pharmaceutical industry's profit margins began to shrink and thus, they had to reevaluate the way in which they were utilizing their sales forces. Those who understood that survival meant performing at the highest level for motives other than individual achievement or accolades were able to sustain their careers through this tumultuous period.

CHAPTER 5

Empathy

"You can't judge someone until you've walked a mile in their shoes." "Empathy is trying on someone else's shoes – Sympathy—wearing them."

—Unknown

"Peace cannot be achieved through violence, it can only be attained through understanding."

—Albert Einstein

"Leadership is about empathy. It is about having the ability to relate to and connect with people for the purpose of inspiring and empowering their lives."

—Oprah Winfrey

There are countless sayings and famous quotes in the world regarding empathy. This concept has been drilled into us since we were young. Often, mothers instruct their children to "be nice to the other kids in class today, okay?" and cite empathy if the kid is mean—"how would you feel if *you* were the new kid and everyone was mean to you?" Teachers explain its relevance when discussing differences among cultures and lessons in racial harmony. Therefore, it's a very familiar lesson, but people utilize it too infrequently in today's society. People as a whole easily get caught up in their own events, their own lives, their own upbringing, and their own perspectives. Even if it isn't explicitly "all about me," it really becomes that way if we're not conscious of the tendency to be self-absorbed. After all, it's human nature.

As with the overarching idea of Emotional Intelligence itself, empathy is a practice. It isn't always natural to immediately open our minds to other possibilities. Our own upbringing and culture is so intrinsic to us, so entangled with what we are as individuals, that it is difficult sometimes to consider others' differences. And a major human habit is to dislike that which is different. That disdain for differences is why ethnic cleansing, genocide, racism, sexism, and the plethora of discriminatory practices exist. A lack of empathy is extremely commonplace in the world, unfortunately. It *can* be practiced and improved, though, with a strong desire. Like Emotional Intelligence, willingness to acquire its skills is vital in acquiring it at all.

According to Daniel Goleman, empathy is the "ability to consider others' feelings, especially when making decisions...the ability to connect with others, even when different from your own perspectives" (2004). As with many of the aspects of Emotional Intelligence, this requires ou to stop and think (probably thinking more before you act) and step outside of your comfort zone. Even if it's unnatural to *not* think of yourself first, this is what empathy dictates. Consider where others come from and how they must feel. As the saying goes, "perception is reality." This means their understanding is just as accurate to them as your understanding is fact to you.

Empathy is the ability to experience and relate to the thoughts, emotions, or experiences of others. Empathy is more than simple sympathy, which is being able to understand and support others with compassion or sensitivity. In fact, unlike the typically sweet and feeling aspects of sympathy, empathy has the tendency to be "tough." Tough empathy is "giving people what they need, not what they want" (Goffee et al. 2000).

While it is important to be aware of others' backgrounds and opinions, the project at hand takes precedence. This doesn't mean we abandon empathy in favor of a project, or spend *all* of our time listening to other people. Tough empathy is a balancing act. Leaders must know when it's appropriate and helpful, and how much time to devote to it.

Many leadership theories suggest the ability to have and display empathy is a fundamental part of leadership. Transformational leaders need empathy in order to show their followers that they care for their needs and achievement (Bass, 1985). Authentic leaders also need to have empathy in order to be aware of others (Walumbwa, Avolio, Gardner, Wernsing, & Peterson, 2008). Empathy is a key part of emotional intelligence that several researchers believe is critical to being an effective leader (Bar-On & Parker, 2000; George, 2000; Goleman, 1995; Salovey & Mayer, 1990).

Consider language tutors, for instance. If an American writing consultant at a university writing center is working with a Chinese international student, chances are that they have different views of how their dynamics should be. Because the American tutor is also a student, he just views this as an informal service for his peers and wants to get chummy during his consultations. However, the international student is taught in his culture that this is an instance requiring respect toward an authority figure—the tutor has more knowledge than him regarding English writing skills. As a result, the Chinese student shows respect in the way he knows how: by averting his gaze, by acting quiet and submissive. The American tutor is perplexed. *Why are Chinese students so antisocial*, he wonders. *Did I say something wrong? I'm trying to be nice.* As the session goes on, the tutor just assumes there is "something wrong" with the student, and that he's an unfriendly guy.

The differences don't cease there. The tutor views the essay they're working on improving together as hopeless. The perspective of the essay jumps from person to person, and it's hard to keep track. In actuality, this is because Asian cultures "are told to approach a topic from a variety of viewpoints…to a U.S. trained tutor, this might indicate lack of focus" (Shanti et al. 2004). The tutor becomes frustrated and doesn't ask about what the writer was going for in his essay. Instead, he swiftly corrects him and lectures about how unfocused it is. "Choose one perspective. I don't really get what you're trying to do here. Just cross it out." If the tutor paid attention, he could see the student shifting in his seat uncomfortably. The student wants to explain his reasoning but doesn't think it's appropriate or that he even has the vocabulary to clearly explain his train of thought.

In both instances, the tutor thought his perception was reality, not just *his* personal reality. The fact the student was not talking much meant that the student was shy or unfriendly, no ifs ands or buts. The essay dilemma was similar in that the tutor felt there was only one logical way to organize a paper, and the Chinese student fell short of that standard. Really, there was a method to the "madness," and the Chinese student was excelling according to his cultural requirements.

If the tutor had taken culture into account, he would have handled the situation different. Ideally, he would have considered previous students he had worked with—maybe he'd have noticed a trend in many Asian students' treatment of the tutor/student dynamic. With friends, they're sociable and louder, but once the tutor session starts, he might have noticed the abrupt switch in demeanor. He could have even asked, "What do you think about this section?" or "Tell me why you wrote this paragraph about her perspective." Asking questions, if done tactfully, shows an interest in learning another perspective and humbly addresses the fact that one doesn't have all the answers. The same idea goes for the essay; the tutor could have asked, "What was your thought process in regards to the organization?" This reveals an openness that ultimately may have led the tutor to understand the perspective of the student. The lesson then could have gone in a more global direction—the tutor could have addressed the problem and made a general statement about organization in American versus Chinese academic papers for the Chinese student's future essays. Then he would have in turn gained a greater understanding of what's expected in American practices, improving the learning environment in this session as a whole on *both* sides. In short, the tutor needed to put himself in his peer's shoes. *It's difficult to live in a foreign country, let alone write in another language,* he could have reasoned. *Let me make this easier for him. I know I would be very timid too.*

This situation involves just one of the many environments that benefit from a strong desire for empathy. According to Executive Diversity Services, Inc: zzzzz [block quote] On the deepest level, empathy requires a willingness to suspend our own perspective and plans long enough to really take in where the other person is coming from. Keen observation and active listening are two of the most powerful tools a leader can employ in developing empathy.

("Emotional Intelligence: A Promising Pathway to Inclusion" 2010) zzzzz-end [block quote] In doing this, maybe the tutor would have noticed by the facial features of the student that something was amiss. Maybe he would have noticed hesitance or a sense of confusion in the student's facial features. Noticing such nuances would help prompt the discussion necessary for learning and understanding.

As could be expected, in order to notice these hard-to-pick-up signs, you must be looking out for them, you must *care*. A lot of situations requiring empathy won't be obvious, so active looking and listening, usually as a result of attention and carefulness, is a must. According to the book *Cultural Intelligence: Learning and Working Globally Second Edition*, there are three skills that work toward developing cultural intelligence, or a flexibility in interacting with other cultures. These are *knowledge*, or awareness of a culture, what that culture consists of, and the similarities and differences in relation to your own culture. Next is *mindfulness*, which is touched upon earlier in the paragraph.

This entails the attention and care one devotes to picking up on cultural cues, utilizing their knowledge (Thomas et al. 2009). Eventually, the knowledgeable and mindful person will gain *cross-cultural skills*. By putting the other two steps into practice, a culturally intelligent person demonstrates competence in a wide variety of interactions (Thomas et al. 2009).

Because the people of the world today are more connected in a global community thanks to technological advancements and globalization, empathy is hugely applicable in matters of culture. It is then important to analyze globalization and its impact in the workplace.

Globalization

Globalization penetrates almost every area of life, even though many people don't consciously think about it as the large force that it is. When you go to the grocery store, globalization is omnipresent: you have potatoes, yams, and corn from South America, bananas from Asia, Africa, and generally tropical areas, sugar from the Caribbean, rice from Asia, and so on. Even historically, food has different origins than one would originally assume. Although the Irish are associated with the potato, it was brought over by explorers from South America. Tomatoes were thought to be poisonous in Britain, where it is now heartily enjoyed today. McDonalds is the symbol of America's value of efficiency even when it comes to food, yet McDonalds are virtually everywhere. Take an airplane to Italy and you'll find a McDonalds nestled beside a family-owned pizza shop.

And food is just one category. Globalization is present when MTV appears on Spaniards' and Middle Easterners' television sets. It's how Snoopy appears on Japanese kids' t-shirts and how Pokémon arrived in the United States. It's why French fashions catch on in many posh places in the world. It's why it's a wise idea to take a business Chinese course in college. On that note, it's not unusual for businesses to make international conference calls to India, China, and areas in the far corners of the world. People expand their businesses in other parts of the world, such as Walmart bringing its stores to China. Globalization is a force to be reckoned with; it's the phenomenon that brings us our standard of living.

Globalization is defined as "the increase of permeability of traditional boundaries, not just those of business organizations but those around countries, economies, industries, and people" (Thomas et al. 2009). This is attributed to a variety of factors. Increased interconnectedness internationally, the rise in human migration, and the ease and rapidity of information transfer—no matter the distance—are causes of a global village (Thomas et al. 2009). Then it is no wonder why employees of a business, and in particular the managers and leaders higher up, should have competent empathetic skills. As shown in the Writing Center example, even the seemingly simple interaction of an international student requesting help from a native peer on an essay is a chance for myriad miscommunications. Taking the world of business to an international level, then, creates endless possibilities for misunderstanding. It is thus more necessary than ever before for leaders to acquaint themselves with the right knowledge, a high level of mindfulness, and overall developing sufficient cross-cultural skills in this global environment.

Culture is a primary challenge when communicating across the world. For example, the daily schedule in Spain versus America seems almost antithetical. While Americans are up at six a.m. to brew a cup of joe and to beat the morning traffic, Spaniards begin their mornings far later (their eight a.m. is as bustling as our six a.m.). Breakfast in Spain is usually around nine a.m.—usually only a slice of bread and jam because American breakfasts are considered too protein-heavy and rich—and then they wait until two or three o'clock in the afternoon for lunch so it matches up with their siesta. Families join together mid-afternoon to eat a large meal, more equivalent to our concept of supper. This lunch/siesta lasts a leisurely two hours. Then they return to work until eight o'clock at night. It's not unusual for a ten o'clock p.m. dinner (which is much lighter than an American dinner). Their days are stretch out into their nights. Overall they are more of a culture of "night owls" than here; the sun doesn't fully set until around ten p.m. Because of this more drawn-out (some may perceive as "relaxed") schedule, other cultures may perceive the Spanish as "lazy." Talk to a Spaniard, though, and they may call Americans too uptight, stressed, and fat as a result. To Spaniards, they see themselves as enjoying life and appreciating family time and gastronomy. Meals are at home so they can catch up on their day and enjoy food with those that matter the most, not in a rushed manner at their desks at work.

Both Spanish and American lifestyles make sense and have their own rationale.

They are just different and reveal varying values among the cultures. When working with those of another culture, there are considerations that one wouldn't even expect. Even tiny tasks like scheduling important events, conference calls, and so on, rely on knowledge of daily routines and values. It's hard to predict what should be taken into consideration in cross-cultural communications. Daily routines, values, gestures, body language, and just about anything to take into account in a globalized world highly benefits and even requires a strong sense of empathy to show respect for and work with these differences.

Real-Life Applications

Empathy is one critical factor in relationships. In sales or any other business that requires customer interactions, relationships—that are a direct result of empathy—are essential for understanding the needs and desires of your clients. As a leader in sales and marketing and involved in developing strategies to introduce to products to physicians, it was imperative that I supported opportunities for the sales team to experience what their customers would endure day-to-day given our product promotional disease state.

Because of the changes that occurred in the pharmaceutical sales industry during the past fifteen years, doctors are now under a tremendous amount of pressure to now not only write prescriptions because of clinical benefits, but also because of costs. They were hoax-writing left and right to prescribe certain products. When it came to pharmaceutical sales, if doctors knew we weren't covered under, say, United Healthcare, this would be frustrating for them. In the past, they would write off the best product. Pharmaceutical salespeople didn't mention if the drug was covered under second-tier, Blue Cross Blue Shield, and so on. The focus was instead on the quality of the product, and the salespeople emphasized that this was the product the doctors would need.

However, once the doctors wrote it off to the patients, patients would encounter problems with the insurance compatibility and would say, "Hey, I'm at the pharmacy and can't even get the product I need!" The patient might have been on Blue Cross and Blue Shield while the product is covered on United Healthcare, for instance. These experiences blindsided the doctors. The days of all the products being covered ended, and the products shifted—along with the thought processes of the salespeople—to the point where not all products were covered under one plan.

People like myself in pharmaceutical sales realized they had to change the way they sold to customers. The former status quo no longer succeeded. To combat the issues of conflicting insurance plans with the products, we commenced the use of formulary cards. With these cards, we would show doctors ten different plans—Cigna, Blue Cross Blue Shield, and so on. Now we could show doctors where products are covered on each plan and the approximate copays for each plan. On top of that, I wanted to get through to the sales representatives that they had to be more comprehensive in helping physicians procure the best access to our products. We made sure they understood where they would get the least resistance to prescribe products.

This was an excellent solution, but it was not sufficient. Paired with the new formulary cards, pharmaceutical salespeople needed to wield empathy. Preceptorships are a great assistance in this venture. I stressed if we know we're not covered under a certain insurance, such as United Healthcare, and sell without consideration to that, this will later only be frustrating to physicians. We have to be aware of the situation—that many patients have said the doctor wrote this product because they wanted more money, or so it would seem because it's not covered under their plan. So it's vital that the sales representatives know what physicians encounter on a day-to-day basis. They need to sympathize after the doctor complains. They need to walk in their shoes. Doctors will want to know about the cost of the drug and the availability to patients. Unless my reps are aware of situations such as these, it will be hard to see eye-to-eye with the doctors and secure a solution that leaves both the doctors and the reps satisfied.

The scenario might go something like this:

"I just wanted to let you know about [such and such product] and its benefits…"

"No. I don't want this unless it's covered under each insurance plan of my patients. Aetna, Cigna, Blue Cross and Blue Shield…I have quite a few." The doctor is short and doesn't want to cope with angry patients anymore. "Do you think your product will work with everyone? I highly doubt it."

"Yes, I know that's a big concern for you—as it should be. But—"

"Let me tell you a bit about how this went with you guys last time. I had a patient call me and he couldn't get the medicine he needed. He called me 'money-hungry.' Said I'm making deals with you people who only care about the profits. I'm not having any of it."

"Sir, I know that's frustrating. And that's not how it should be. We want to make you guys better informed, so we've developed formulary cards for this purpose. Please just take a look, and you can see that it will help."

The discussion wouldn't stop there, but as you can already tell, the salesperson had to put his pitch on pause in favor of hearing the doctor out. He had to discover where the doctor was coming from, and show that he cared and understood. He'd later go on to say, "I wouldn't want to deal with that either..." and peppered various phrases in to show he identified with the doctor's situation and wanted to improve it as a result.

When empathy is active in situations such as these, the customer will feel cared for and better understood. This builds trust. When trust is high, there will be a more cooperative relationship—the customer will leave with a better experience, and the salesperson is more likely to make their sale. Sympathy is simply not enough. Everybody has their own path they've walked, and therefore have their own reasons for their opinions and approaches. Show that you respect the experiences of others by employing empathy in your daily interactions.

CHAPTER 6

Social Skills

According to Emotional Intelligence pioneer, Daniel Goleman, "the leader's task is to get work done through other people" (2004). Let's hone in on one phrase in particular: *other people*. To effectively lead, the inclusion and harnessing of other people is essential. Leaders do not sit alone all day doing paperwork, making excel spreadsheets, and working on the whole project single-handedly. They are the forces of mobilization.

The necessity of getting "work done through other people" contains the inherent quality of social skills, or successfully working with other people to bring projects to fruition.

Think of the effective leaders of the world and the CEOs of companies. While chances are that their technical skills in their field are excellent, that's not the only reason they climbed to the top of the business ladder. They utilize effective social skills. Steve Jobs, Bill Gates, Randall L. Stephenson of AT&T, Larry Page of Google, and other CEOs of familiar corporations no doubt fit the criteria (remember, Steve Jobs didn't even go to college!). Managing a company and all its employees is no job for the antisocial—imagine the difficulties that would arise if the CEO had no desire to work with people!

How would the company goals be carried out with leaders who couldn't communicate them?

Social skills in the workplace entail a variety of abilities, most of which are predictable: being able to strike up a conversation, good listening skills, and showing an enjoyment for social activities in the first place. Those are a given. In the workplace, social skills range from networking, directing and managing people toward a goal, building rapport with anybody that crosses your path, and harnessing the aforementioned skills of self-awareness, self-regulation, and empathy. Indeed, social skills are the culmination of the other components of Emotional Intelligence.

Imagine if a person fancied herself as having great social abilities but didn't excel in the other areas of Emotional Intelligence. For instance, she loves to chat, but she isn't self-aware enough to know when she's talking too much—or when it's apparent that her coworkers are sick of listening to her gab. Maybe she's a friendly person, but if she lacks this awareness, she'll come off as annoying. Another person could be bubbly and help others come out of their shell. Her downfall is that she doesn't know how to calm down and get a hold on herself when she's stressed out, thereby stressing out everybody around her. Then they don't want to cross her path when any major deadlines approach because she's out of control. If a person isn't empathetic, they can't tell in either instance how those around them feel in those respective situations. If a leader can't express empathy, how would those around them know that he possesses it at all? In looking at these scenarios, if you lacked in one area of the five facets of Emotional Intelligence, people would laugh in your face if you fancied that you actually did have excellent social skills.

To better picture an emotionally intelligent leader who particularly exemplifies social skills, think about Doug. Doug is a manager at his branch of the company, and it's no coincidence or stroke of luck that he is one of the youngest managers in the company's history. Ever since he was a senior in college, he demonstrated that he knows how to network. He had attended job fairs and mastered them, building rapport with the employers instantly. "People love to talk about themselves," he always said. " Give them a chance to talk about themselves, and your relationship will be richer." Indeed, he always asked employers how they got to where they were, what they had majored in, and questions that showed sincere interest and allowed for responses demonstrating admiration and appreciation. When it came to the interviews, he planned stories that highlighted his skills best, such as when he had to get really creative before finals week to accomplish all of his tasks, or times he had to work with people he didn't necessarily like. After he secured the job, he carried over an awareness of how to talk with people (and, quite frankly, make them like you), how to talk about his skills realistically, and "own" the skills that are strongest.

The first couple years of his job, he made sure to get to know his coworkers, from the receptionist to the IT guy and everybody in between. Even if just for a moment, he wanted there to be a meaningful exchange between his coworkers and himself. This helped his coworkers to view him as a jovial, genuine guy, even if they didn't know him too personally. Not only did Doug do this but he also applied his knowledge of his tendencies that he garnered from his job search to take on extra projects through which he knew he could excel, and admit his faults and cope with them. He knew he had a tendency to become bored easily, so planned out times in his agenda to delegate to different tasks during the day—at least he knew when he'd be working on what and could keep track of these changes.

As time wore on, he continued to rise in the company. Soon he began conducting interviews. He always knew to ask the right questions that determined the best candidates. Plus, he knew how to put people at ease, not just in the context of interviews, but with everyone he met. This was really good for working with customers and sales. By paying attention to subtleties in body language and facial expressions, Doug could tell if someone was uncomfortable, nervous, angry, or stressed, and responded appropriately.

This came in handy for public speaking, too. Once he had a presentation at the very end of the day, right before their Christmas party, and many of the employees were impatient for it to end. Adjusting to his audience, he began the speech with, "I know we all want to enjoy Pamela's brownies—myself included! But if you listen to what I have to say, I know we can all benefit from these points before we head off to the Christmas party." He related with the audience and knew how they must feel. By acknowledging this, he gained people's interest and seemed down-to-earth (while still recognizing that his presentation is important). Tactics such as these always demonstrated Doug's social skills and adaptability in any situation.

Social skills are more than you immediately assume, even though they encompass familiar skills. The ability to talk and listen to others is involved, of course—but it's a blend of other Emotional Intelligence skills, as Doug shows. Without the ability to be self-aware, to self-regulate, and empathize, social skills are not up to the optimum level. But aside from that, social skills is much deeper than solely being sociable, as it's often mistaken to primarily be. Social skills are relationship management. Not only that but the ability to manage relationships to move people in a desired direction. Viewing social skills as managing your relationships as opposed to sociability will help ou view *how* you communicate with somebody (not just the fact you're communicatin at all). If you realize you have to keep the relationship in tact, you would take a different approach to maintaining that relationship. For instance, in a salesperson/prospective customer relationship, the ultimate goal isn't to be friends and have a conversation for a while. It's to make a sale. Keeping that in mind, you will want to transition the relationship to one involving a potential customer to a relationship with an actual customer. To do that, attention must be paid to what is said and how it is said. If you were trying to sell a phone at Radio Shack, you wouldn't say, "Hey, you. Buy this phone." You'd try a more subtle approach so as to not bombard the customer. "Hey, what are you out shopping for today?" is a more casual, natural means of opening a conversation. Not only that, but being robotic isn't going to snag a sale. A customer is more likely to be open to a personable, authentic employee. Then it's not just a pawn of the company, it's a fellow person who wants the best for you (if you can interact just right).

Likewise, if a manager of a company is trying to make a business proposition to a prospective partner overseas, it's a more delicate situation than being nice and approachable. Each word the manager makes either advances or hurts the case for the proposition. But that brings us to our next point.

Social Across Cultures

What entails decent social skills in America? You may envision people at a typical American bar with a blonde serving drinks to an array of customers in front of her. Yes, she makes her tips by providing prompt service and paying attention to the needs of her clientele. But she delivers an entirely new experience by smiling, laughing at what others may perceive as terrible jokes, and knowing what to say when and why. In other words, she has social skills. You wouldn't hire a bartender that is indecipherable from a reclusive hermit in a cave, would you? One who stares into space and doesn't talk to people unless it's to respond to a yes or no question? That would be very off-putting, and not good for a business.

However, keep in mind that a smiling, laughing, chatty person who politely asks questions about someone else's day is what American culture conceives good social skills to be. But take Russian culture: unwarranted smiling, for example, is highly unusual.

Russians believe that if you have nothing substantial to smile about, why do it? Otherwise you just look insane. If you went to Russia and saw crowds of its unsmiling, serious-looking inhabitants, you might have thought, *What's up with everybody here? They have no social skills. Everyone is intimidating, and I feel unwelcome.* Keep in mind that the culture is different, and their reasoning makes sense in its own way. In America, smiling—even at people you haven't met—shows you're a happy-go-lucky, approachable person. In Russia, it's unnecessary and doesn't make sense. Perhaps consider Russia's history; it's not the happiest place in the world with its famines, communism, dictators, and wars. The smiling concept might have been an outlook that arose from a series of unhappy times. To each his own, and the same idea goes for social practices in various cultures.

The opportunity to reveal true social prowess is when you interact with other cultures. Summoning your skills of self-awareness, self-regulation, motivation, and empathy, you have the tools you nee to be social in a sensitive context. By paying attention to how other cultures act, you can infer their thoughts on American actions. Cultures that are modest, family-oriented, or more reflective potentially view us as loud, selfish, and rash by comparison. To create common ground, you can do as they do—pay attention to their mannerisms and self-regulate accordingly. Think: *am I much louder than everyone else in the room? Am I the only person asking questions during this presentation? If so, perhaps it's a good idea to sit back for a while. I notice people are bowing when they greet one another. I might have to do that too. People are eating their lunch in this manner—I'll imitate them.* The situations are endless. Be aware of yourself and your situation, think from their point of view instead of acting hastily or becoming angry, and act according to these customs you witness. As with other practices of Emotional Intelligence, know that you will make mistakes every so often. But showing a willingness to interact under other cultures' terms and pay attention to them are signs of respect. This may earn you respect as well. By no means are these tasks as easy as one, two, three. But thinking along these lines can be a helpful start.

Real-Life Application

People seem to know intuitively that leaders need to manage relationships effectively; no leader is an island. As a sales manager in the pharmaceutical industry, coaching sales representative in the field once every six weeks or so, I realized how valuable this time was. I had to balance the time I spent coaching skill sets and time getting to know them and find out how they were doing on a personal level. As a leader it is always in the back of your mind that you have to manage relationships to have the ability to move people in a desired direction. People will not follow any leader until a leader can demonstrate that he cares.

At many points in someone's career, you need people to perform tasks that they may not be interested in. You ask them to do it because it's in the best interest of the venture. However, you cannot expect someone to do this unless you show that you're looking out for their best interests personally. To do this, you can't demonstrate what the corporation says all the time—it's robotic and impersonal. You have to have transparent conversations with people—understand what they want and work that into the organization's goals. Sometimes these do not necessarily go together. At this point, show the employee how the company's goals will help them grow as a person. As the leader, come up with a plan to help the employee reach those goals.

Even when you're at work, don't spend all day talking business with the employees. I always try to ask my reps how they're doing personally, and if there's anything I can do to help them. This also functions as part of a retention strategy. If you want to keep your best employees in an organization, you must use social skills to manage the relationship. This is where social skills and sociability differ—social skills move your relationships in a desired direction and involve a plan, a purpose. Sociability, on the other hand, is lackadaisical and artificial in comparison. The strategy involved in social skills isn't present in simple sociability. I never invite employees drinking for this reason; the activity tends to signify sociability rather than purposeful interaction and an opportunity to show the person that they are valuable.

In realizing that your employees are valuable and bring a purpose to your venture, you don't need to be fake in social situations. When you realize that you need somebody in your organization, you sincerely want to know and care about that person. For me, it's easier to stay in tune with that person. I'll want to text them and ask, "What's going on out there?" Likewise, I show them I value their opinion by asking for them.

Another important application for social skills is reaching out to families. When I reach out to the representatives to connect with them, I always try to take them and their spouse out to dinner. The reason I invite their families is because it shows I don't just care about the employee, I care about their biggest support system. The demands of the sales work schedule separates families, so I know that the employee is making a family sacrifice by choosing to work in my business. The spouse needs to know that the manager/leader empathizes with that as a fellow family-oriented person.

In these ways, you can utilize social skills. It's all about moving people in a desired direction by drawing upon the previous four facets of Emotional Intelligence. Your social skills are not up to par if you cannot wield each facet mentioned earlier in the book. Likewise, social skills are markedly different from sociability in that they involve purposeful interaction, which lead your venture to intended results.

CHAPTER 7

More Leadership Post-EI development

You've done it: you learned and continue to practice each feature of Emotional Intelligence. You have a handle on self-awareness, self-regulation, motivation, empathy, and social skills, and you know what practicing each skill entails. There's always room for improvement in the area of Emotional Intelligence, so there's never a point at which someone could deem his or herself an expert. It's a lifelong practice that will never cease to increase your success in whatever position you may hold. However, there are various applications for Emotional Intelligence. One application is the navigation of the different leadership styles. You may think that utilizing all these features of Emotional Intelligence will lead to one definite leadership style. That is simply not the case. There are different combinations of Emotional Intelligence skills that comprise a leadership style; each one is fitting for a different situation. If you were a teacher, you'd know there isn't just one way to teach because students learn in a variety of ways. The same idea applies here.

There are different ways to lead because different people and different situations require different strategies.

There are six leadership styles that, if you have a firm grasp on Emotional Intelligence and practice them enough, you can seamlessly weave into your repertoire of skills. You will be able to distinguish when it is best to use these styles, which facets of Emotional Intelligence are needed, and with whom to use them. The six leadership styles include the coercive, authoritative, affiliative, democratic, pacesetting, and coaching styles. Sometimes a couple of these (coercive and pacesetting styles) are to be used with caution: they are only beneficial in a handful of situations and should therefore only be used selectively. The other four of the six styles, though, will benefit the workplace when used appropriately. After all, it has been shown that effective leadership—leadership that utilizes styles that positively affected the office environment—is related to higher financial results (Goleman 2000). As previously stated with the implementation of Emotional Intelligence in leadership, not only will there be results financially, as every business strives for, but the job performance and the overall morale of the employees will increase too. Knowing that, we're going take a quick look at each style and the pros and cons as described by the Emotional Intelligence pioneer, Daniel Goleman.

Coercive Style

Think of somebody in control—and everybody knows it. Everybody is to follow that person's orders at once, no more, no less. If you envision one of those slave ships where ten men are on one oar, rowing to the beat of the leader's drum, the situation is quite similar. Daniel Goleman says this style can be boiled down to the phrase "Do what I say" (Goleman 2000).

It sounds harsh. You may wonder how any situation necessitates the usage of such a style. Keep in mind that it should only be used in extreme situations. If you want to change the company culture, commence a turnaround, or are leading employees through an emergency, this is the best option. What else would you use if the building was on fire and you had to lead your employees through the crisis? Certainly that wouldn't be a coaching situation.

Consider another example: Michelle is the director of the Learning and Teaching program at a university. She works closely with the provost and occasionally the university president. She's told that a new building is in the works for her department, which she views as the perfect opportunity to conduct a turnaround: the one who previously held her position was strict and closed, and it showed. She states the need for many windows in her building so it's less dark and feels "less like a dungeon." She begins with the minute details of her own office's look and then, the department. Conference tables are replaced with round, circular tables to create a feeling of inclusiveness. The room is painted a warm shade of brown sugar. There are more bookshelves to create an aura of learning and collaboration. She overlooks this process and explains what she wants in detail because it's in the best interest of the university. In the end, this is successful: more students and staff feel welcome, so they come to utilize the department's services more often.

Except in these situations, the coercive style rarely yields positive results. With someone directing you and expecting you to follow orders, there's less room for creativity. The morale of employees lowers because they don't feel they have any responsibility or that their thoughts are important (Goleman 2000). If the situation doesn't call for coerciveness, you'll only appear bossy and like a control-freak.

Authoritative Style

This tends to be the most positive leadership style, and is great when a company lacks direction. As stated in the first chapter, a leader is expected to deliver a vision and get results. The authoritative style effectively does this by utilizing the Emotional Intelligence feature of motivation. Daniel Goleman explains that this style can be summed up in the phrase "Come with me." Authoritative leaders set a goal and enthusiastically motivate the team to reach it with them.

"We need to make a change—computers could and should be in every home in America. Let's make them smaller, more affordable, and easy to understand." Bill Gates might have said something like this to Microsoft to get the ball rolling on personal computers. This gave the company a goal, something to look to. Efforts were then directed to make this happen.

There are few situations when this is inappropriate, but Goleman says that if there is a team of experienced professionals nearby who know more about the situation than the leader at hand, then the authoritative leader should step back. Otherwise they will appear "pompous and overbearing" (Goleman 2000). If the leader is the expert, then they can feel free to inspire the team with a vision and the means to reach it. Unlike the coercive style, the team possesses the freedom to attain the goal in the means they prefer. The leader primarily breathes fresh air into the organization and maps a new path.

Affiliative

"People come first" is what an affiliative leader would say (Goleman 2000). An affiliative leader values the interactions with their employees, wanting to get to know them and connect with them to create a bond. This utilizes the features of social skills and a large degree of motivation. Using these skills creates an environment of harmony and lets the employee feel cared for. Unlike in the coercive style, where bosses appear robotic and stringent, affiliative leaders allow themselves to appear human, and they take the liberty to be more open. They may mention their situation at home, like having a sick baby.

This is valuable for bosses who wish to gain the trust of their employees and get to know them more personally. The open environment that results puts employees at ease and boosts their sense of a community spirit. People work better with those that they are comfortable around and can trust. They feel they can share their ideas and work with less stress.

As I mentioned from my personal experiences in the pharmaceutical industry, I used social skills to get to know my sales representatives. The steps I took—inviting families to dinner, talking frankly about their career goals, and simply asking how it's going—all fit under the criteria of this affiliative style.

A downside to this approach is that "bad practices go uncorrected," as stated by Goleman. Praise is important in boosting morale, not to mention it is rare in today's society. There needs to be some sort of emphasis on what to improve, what could be better. Forgoing constructive criticism causes employees to lose valuable opportunities to reach their highest potential. Each practice has its place in the world of business. To combat this problem, affiliative style is used in conjunction with the authoritative style to create a purpose for the positivity endorsed here.

Democratic Style

You can easily guess the characteristics of this style if you think about the American democracy and ancient Greek politics. This style allows for participation and discussion, and it serves as a forum for the exchange of ideas. Again, the employees feel respected and comfortable to share their own ideas. Social skills and self-regulation is prominent here, social skills because it's important to know how to express yourself and self-regulation because it's easy to get carried away or become upset when opposing ideas surface.

How many times have you sat in a meeting that dragged on and on, seemingly without a purpose and any structure? This is a possible downside of the democratic structure. It's important that the participants are informed, that it's clear that an end goal needs to be reached, and that it stays on topic. If a leader knows the end goal, then it's pointless to hear everybody's opinions as well.

Suppose there's a problem, such as not meeting financial goals. The democratic style allows for the employees to give input, exposing the leader to various options he might not have considered. Hearing the ideas of employees is time consuming, but it will create more trust and a feeling of worth in employees.

Pacesetting

As with the coercive style, pacesetting is best used sparingly. Goleman sums it as "Do as I do now." Essentially it's a style that reveals a preoccupation with perfection and/or improvement. The pacesetting leader would find people who aren't performing as well as they could and then try to make them improve by following their example or replacing them altogether. Not a fun scenario as it stresses employees out, making them obsess over the way they work.

When employees are self-motivated, competent, and competitive, pacesetting gives them the nudge they need to set off for a new direction (Goleman 2000). This utilizes motivation to a high extent, as can be seen, and has the potential to refresh the team with a new way of performing. Otherwise the working environment is bleak because the employees' morale is so low and the boss is seen as a micromanager.

To see how it functions, take a look at this scenario: Korri is the product manager at a local, fashionable retail store. She wants to meet her segment's sales goals more frequently so decides to employ new tactics. She starts with the front of the store and will make her way to the back. At the front is the greeter, Mallory.

"Hi, how are you doing? Welcome to the store," Mallory says, looking up from her clothes-folding to flash a smile to the newcomers.

The customers say they're good and start to peruse the selection of yoga pants in the store. Korri decides to accost Mallory once the customers are out of earshot.

"Mallory, what happened over there?"

Mallory appears confused. "I'm not sure...what do you mean?" "What was wrong with that picture? What *didn't* you do?"

Mallory thinks for a second, biting her lip. "I guess I could have asked what I could help them with?"

"Right," says Korri. "You didn't ask what you could help them with. Engage them in open-ended questions. Do you know what those are?"

"Questions that don't result in a yes or no answer?" "Mmhmm. Now try this again."

Korri watches Mallory as new customers stroll into the store. She says hello, welcome to the store, and if there's anything she can help them with today. The customer says no, and Mallory replies with, "Oh, okay. Cool. Just let me know!" Korri is exasperated with the response and walks up to Mallory again when the customers move toward the back of the store.

"Mallory, what did you do wrong?"

"I thought I did it right? I did what you told me to..."

"Yes, but you didn't let them know about the great deals we have in the store today! Sometimes when customers are 'just looking,' they aren't aware of the sales. Let them know if they say they're 'just looking' so they'll change their minds and buy something."

"Okay, what are the sales?"

Korri gives a rundown on three different in-store promotions for Mallory to keep in mind. "Now, so this is easier for you, I'm going to show you how to do this. Then you can try after me."

A middle-aged lady and her mother walk into the store, sipping coffees. Korri walks in front of them and shoots a toothy grin. "Hey ladies! How are you doing today?"

"Fine, thank you," says the mother.

"Excellent. What are you out shopping for today?"

"Oh, we're just looking, thanks." Korri stands in front of them so they give her their full attention.

"Well just so you ladies know, we have so many awesome things going on in the store today! We have new shorts over in this section." Korri points. "And we have a sale buy one get one half off lotions. Would you like me to show you where they are?"

"Sure."

Mallory feels uncomfortable because this is not her preferred method of interacting with customers. She likes to get to know the customers through the duration of their store visit, not instantly bombard them with information. Deciding to tell Korri this respectfully, she will be discouraged.

"No, Mallory. It isn't bombarding the customer. It's doing your job. Now try doing your job like I showed you."

Mallory is clearly aggravated but decides to give it a shot. She sounds nervous and feels unnatural, but she does what Korri says.

There's a time and place for pacesetting. It's also imperative that the leader doesn't carp at the employees to the point their morale sinks. In the scenario, Mallory felt she couldn't contribute anything to her customer/employee dynamic. She felt she had to robotically do exactly what Korri said to do at that moment. Now, if pacesetting occurred with a team of technical recruiters—who make commission off of their hires—then this would be appropriate, as they are likely competitive, driven people who could use direct instruction in this specific industry.

Coaching

Just as a coach would do in a sport setting, a coaching leader cajoles the employees to "try this" (Goleman 2000). If a little league baseball player has the strength to hit the ball out of the park repeatedly, but is not using proper technique in swinging the bat (which is helpful in preventing injury), a coach will explain these strengths and weaknesses to the player. "This is what you're doing well, and this is what you can do to be even better," the coach may say.

As with landing a gig in the major leagues, coaching leadership relies on the employee's aspiration (Goleman 2000). If the employee doesn't want the feedback, though, coaching could be seen as pacesetting. Another important note is that the employer needs to be an expert in this topic—as with baseball, you wouldn't want a coach who knows nothing about the sport, can't play himself, or is actually an expert on golf instead. It's crucial that the coaching leader knows what he's talking about from personal experience.

Because coaching relies on explaining strengths and weaknesses, often from somebody who goes to the leader in search of help and improvement, social skills and self-awareness are important. You must know how you come off in talking about the employee's skills because if you aren't sensitive, the employee may tune out. Coaching can be likened to counseling; coaches provide emotional support and discuss the abilities and feelings of the employee.

For example, at Harry's company, he sits with his boss twice annually to discuss his performance. This isn't a reminder to "step it up," but a chance for the employees to share their experiences, both successes and failures, and talk about how to progress.

Harry ponders for a moment when his boss asks him about his areas of greatest improvement. "This quarter I grew in my abilities to listen to the customer more."

"We've seen a lot of growth in that area as well," his boss says.

"What I really want to learn to do, though, is improve on presentation skills. I know the opportunities don't happen *too* often for me to present research, but I want to step it up and seek out opportunities because I think I have a lot to offer."

"Well, that's simple. We have a few resources to recommend to you, which are..." and the bosses give him a list. "But really, we know you're charismatic, you talk loudly and clearly, so just focus on nonverbal cues more."

The session is a chance for the managers and Harry to connect, but it's beneficial to both parties. Harry brags about himself and receives a pat on the back, but he's also given resources for further improvement with friendly suggestions. This is just one example of a coaching scenario, but they can also occur in five-minute spurts in the middle of a shift, whether in pep talks or side notes.

This style seems too time consuming to many employers. It does require that a leader stops focusing on the work and focuses on the person, but the results are rewarding. Employees thrive and feel satisfied knowing they're being cared for and know how to improve while keeping strengths in mind.

The Distinction of Leadership

Regardless of which aspect of Emotional Intelligence you're focusing on, what leadership style you currently use, where you work, and what your exact leadership position is, there are certain characteristics that are central to leadership to bear in mind. To better understand them, we must contrast it with management.

The first idea for leaders to keep in mind is the primary difference between management and leadership. John P. Kotter defines them as follows: "management is about coping with complexity, it brings order and predictability to a situation...leadership, then, is about learning to cope with rapid change" (1990). He continues to say that management is more control-oriented and deductive in nature, but leadership is an inductive practice.

Why is this? For one, management focuses on planning and budgeting whereas leaders move people in a direction. As you can gather, the former is more precise and detail oriented while the latter focuses on the big picture. Once executives in a business understand this, they can use the two concepts in complement with one another and understand what they are doing with greater clarity.

Once this is accomplished, executives better gauge how to act upon situations.

Management's style dictates a plan with details. But leadership should involve less control. To better cope with change, employees need energy to carry out their tasks without micromanagement. This energy is best attained through leaders' motivation and inspiration—rather than controlling employees. zzzzz- Motivation and inspiration energize people, not by pushing them in the right direction as control mechanisms do but by satisfying basic human needs for achievement, a sense of belonging, recognition, self- esteem, a feeling of control over one's life, and the ability to live up to one's ideals" (Kotter 1990). zzzzz-end If leadership is to direct people in a certain direction, nothing will rev employees' engines like the positive results ("belonging, recognition," and so on, mentioned earlier) engendered by motivation and inspiration.

Sometimes describing a concept alone doesn't give any clarification. But in looking at leadership compared to management, we can certainly see what leadership is and is not. We see where the boundaries are, where leadership begins and ends. While these two concepts at first glance appear similar, they are distinct but complementary in the business world.

CONCLUSION

Every day that you walk through the workplace and see crisp suits and ironed ties, fax machines, conference rooms, and memos, you might think that this is a haven for logic. How would emotions play in the fast-paced world of business? Surely there's no room for it in all the structure and happenings of the office.

This is false. Paying attention to emotions is vital in yielding extraordinary results in not only the business world, but in every setting of life. Knowledge of emotions and the impact they play on your environment is the ingredient for success. Self-awareness, self-regulation, motivation, empathy, and social skills aren't what you hear about in your business class in college; they aren't concepts you cram for before a test and can suddenly wield without issue. These should be everyday practices. You read this book, so you know *about* them, but you do not *know* them just yet. To know these concepts, you must use them—and you must know when and how to use them appropriately.

Emotional Intelligence is vital in leadership, in all styles that are mentioned. If you harness the basic emotional intelligence skills, they will open avenues for you to practice leadership in a variety of ways that are appropriate for whatever situation you confront. The effective leader can effortlessly glide between the styles mentioned above, knowing when each one is appropriate for the given scenario. Not only that, but they know what each style requires—whether empathy to be a successful affiliative leader, or self-awareness to ensure the authoritative style doesn't become coercive. Even after Emotional Intelligence is understood and frequently practiced, there are useful situations in which to use its five facets of self-awareness, self-regulation, motivation, empathy, and social skills.

While Emotional Intelligence is important in any position as a leader, it's particularly important in culture. America is a mosaic of countless cultures from all over the world and sometimes many ethnicities reside in each. On top of that, globalization has increased interaction in the world, namely in the business arena. Technology only speeds up the rate at which people of varying backgrounds and walks of life can interact. Skype video chat, international phone calls, plane rides, the Internet, and countless other forms of technology reduce what should take months to reach somebody across the globe. This leads to endless possibilities for Emotional Intelligence to come in handy, as each culture has its unique "programming" that dictates code of conduct, practices, and behaviors.

These cultural aspects are deeply embedded in its participants, learned and reinforced over the course of their lifetimes. Understanding and open-mindedness in cross-cultural interactions are crucial. They are easier to attain with the help of self-awareness, self- regulation, motivation, empathy, and social skills.

I myself know the value of Emotional and Cultural Intelligence. As a leader in pharmaceutical sales, I can testify that they are integral to the workings of any organization. Self-awareness allows my sales representatives to succeed without my badgering. Self-regulation is not only important on a personal level but company-wide as well. Motivation powers employees to succeed when times are tough. Empathy creates better customer/sales representative relations. Social skills combine all of the above and move people in a purposeful direction. It may not even seem like you're doing them in your day-to-day routine, but in some capacity, you are. Now imagine if you were conscious of each one and knew the optimal time to use them.

Emotional Intelligence opens a world of possibility for success. If you have the commitment to change for the better and practice the five different parts of Emotional Intelligence, your productivity as a leader–and the productivity of your team—will noticeably increase. Intellect is only the first step to leadership prowess. The rest is up to you.

END NOTES

Bielaszka-DuVernay, Christina. "Hiring For Emotional Intelligence." *Harvard Business Press*. (2008).

Peter F. Drucker, "What Makes an Effective Executive?" *Harvard Business Press* (2004).

Executive Diversity Services, Inc, "Emotional Intelligence: A Promising Pathway to Inclusion." Last modified 2010. Accessed May 7, 2012. http://www.executivediversity.com/news/index_eiq.htm.

George, Bill, Peter Sims, Andrew N. McLean, and Diana Mayer. "Discovering Your Authentic Leadership." *Harvard Business Press*. (2007).

Gilkey, Roderick, Ricardo Caceda, and Clinton Kilts. "When Emotional Reasoning Trumps IQ." *Harvard Business Review*. (2010): 1.

Goffee, Robert, and Gareth Jones, "Why Should Anyone Be Led by You?" Harvard Business Press (2000).

Goleman, Daniel. *Emotional Intelligence: Why It Can Matter More Than IQ*. New York: Bantam Books, 1997.

Goleman, Daniel. "Leadership That Gets Results." *Harvard Business Review*. (2000): 16-28.

Goleman, Daniel, Richard Boyatzis, and Annie McKee. "Primal Leadership: The Hidden Driver of Great Performance." *Harvard Business Review*. (2001): 30-41.

Goleman, Daniel. "What Makes a Leader?" *Harvard Business Review.* (2004). 4-12.

Goleman, Daniel. "What Makes a Leader?" *HBR's Ten Top Reads: On Leadership.* Boston: Harvard Business School Publishing Corporation, 2011.

Gupta, Ashim . Practical Management, "Role of an Organizational Leader." Last modified February 2, 2009. Accessed May 7, 2012. http://www.practical-management.com/Leadership-Development/Role-of-an-Organizational-Leader.html.

Heifetz, Ronald, Alexander Grashow, and Marty Linsky. "Engage Courageously: Building the Emotional Awareness and Capacity for Leading Adaptive Change." *The Practice of Adaptive Leadership: Tools and Tactics for Changing Your Organization and the World.* Boston: Harvard Business Press, 2009.

John P. Kotter, "What Leaders Really Do?" *Harvard Business Press* (1990).

Macchiavelli, Niccoló. *The Prince.* Wellesley: Branden Books, 2003.

Prati, L.Melita, Caesar Douglas, Gerald R. Ferris, Anthony P. Ammeter, and M. Ronald Buckley. "Emotional Intelligence, Leadership Effectiveness, and Team Outcomes." *The International Journal of Organizational Analysis.* 11. no. 1 (2003): 21-40.

Salovey, P., & Mayer, J.D. "Emotional Intelligence." *Imagination, Cognition, and Personality,* 9. no. 3 (1990): 185-211.

Shanti, Bruce, and Ben Raforth. *ESL Writers: A Guide for Writing Center Tutors.* Portsmouth, New Hampshire: Boyton/Cook- Heinemann, 2004.

Stibich, PhD, Mark. About.com Health and Longevity, "Top 10 Reasons to Smile." Last modified February 4, 2010.

Accessed May 9, 2012. http://longevity.about.com/od/lifelongbeauty/tp/smiling.htm.

Thomas, David C., and Kerr Inkson. "Mindfulness and Cross- Cultural Skills." *Cultural Intelligence: Living and Working Globally, Second Edition*. Harvard Business Press. (2009).

Thomas, David C., and Kerr Inkson. "Living and Working in the Global Village." *Cultural Intelligence: Living and Working Globally, Second Edition*. (2009).

Thomas, David C., and Kerr Inkson. "Cultural Knowledge." *Cultural Intelligence: Living and Working Globally, Second Edition*. (2009): 20-42. http://cultureofempathy.com/References/Quotes.htm

www.ingramcontent.com/pod-product-compliance
Lightning Source LLC
Chambersburg PA
CBHW030130100526
44591CB00009B/592